A Treatise on Jonathan Edwards Continuous Creation and Christology

A Treatise on Jonathan Edwards Continuous Creation and Christology

By S. Mark Hamilton

Volume 1
A Series of Treatises on Jonathan Edwards

JESociety Press

WWW.JESOCIETY.ORG

Paperback Edition December 11, 2017
ISBN 978-0692975657
© 2017 S. Mark Hamilton

A publication of JESociety Press
Visit http://www.jesociety.org

All rights reserved. No part of this publication may be reproduced, distributed, or transmitted in any form or by any means, including photocopying, recording, or other electronic or mechanical methods, without the prior written permission of the author/publisher, except in the case of brief quotations embodied in critical reviews and certain other noncommercial uses permitted by copyright law.

For permission requests and inquiries,
Email: info@jesociety.org
Web: www.jesociety.org

Cover art: The creation of the world (illustration by Lucas Cranach's workshop in the 1534 edition of Luther's Bible).

A Series of Treatises on Jonathan Edwards

JESociety Press is pleased to announce *A Series of Treatises on Jonathan Edwards*, an all new series given exclusively to the select publication of cutting-edge research related to America's greatest theologian. The series provides authors with a venue for publishing original, concise, authoritative and peer-reviewed manuscripts. The series provides readers with lively, assessable and in-depth treatments of Edwards-specific subject matter. For more information about the series or with questions about JESociety Press, please visit our website at: www.jesociety.org or contact us directly at: info@jesociety.org.

PRAISE FOR THIS VOLUME

Jonathan Edwards was not only America's greatest theologian. He also was its finest early philosopher, but more specifically a prominent philosophical theologian. Among his intriguing—and difficult—contributions to philosophical theology was his doctrine of continuous creation. Its relation to occasionalism has helped and bedeviled thinkers for the last three centuries. No one working on Edwards or philosophical theology should miss Mark Hamilton's careful work on this connection.

Gerald R. McDermott
Anglican Chair of Divinity, Beeson Divinity School,
co-author of *The Theology of Jonathan Edwards*

This is the best attempt to date to systematize the nexus of comments found mainly in Edwards' notebooks on the relationship of ontology, etiology, and Christology. It represents an advance on the account of Hamilton's brilliant teacher, Oliver D. Crisp, one on which analytical minds will noodle for many years to come. I recommend it strongly, and find its arguments for what Hamilton calls Edwards' "immaterial realism" compelling.

Douglas A. Sweeney
Distinguished Professor of Church History and the History of Christian Thought, Trinity Evangelical Divinity School, author of
Edwards the Exegete: Biblical Interpretation and Anglo-Protestant Culture on the Edge of the Enlightenment

In this philosophically dense but highly instructive treatise, Mark Hamilton concludes by admitting that he has "come near the edge of the imponderable." I agree. Jonathan Edwards is known for many things, but few are familiar with what is, in my opinion, the most challenging facet of his thinking: the doctrine of continuous creation. Hamilton has done us a tremendous favor by exploring this notion in great depth and with profound clarity, especially as it relates to Edwards' doctrine of the person of Christ. After working your way through this volume you may conclude that Hamilton has plunged over the edge of the imponderable with little hope of recovery! Perhaps. But you won't regret taking the plunge with him.

Sam Storms
Pastor, Bridgeway Church, author of
Signs of the Spirit: An Interpretation of Jonathan Edwards' "Religious Affections"

Jonathan Edwards's idealism or immaterialism is well known. On the creaturely level, to be is to be perceived. Yet Edwards asserted that the human being is not only perceived but perceiving, and this raises a number of complex issues as to how created minds are distinct from and yet related to the divine Mind, and how created minds and bodies both depend ontologically—and moment-by-moment—on the continuing volition and agency of God as Creator. Mark Hamilton teases out these questions from Edwards's texts with exegetical skill and analytical acumen. Everyone with an interest in Edwards's metaphysical thought ought to take interest in Hamilton's brief treatise on continuous creation and Christology.

Michael McClymond
Professor of Modern Christianity, Saint Louis University,
co-author of *The Theology of Jonathan Edwards*

In this innovative little book, Hamilton shows that Edwards' concept of continuous creation has significant explanatory power regarding the doctrine of Christ. I highly recommend it to anyone interested in Christology or Edwards studies.

James S. Spiegel
Professor of Philosophy and Religion, Taylor University, chief editor of
Idealism and Christianity, Vol. 1: Idealism and Christian Theology & Idealism and Christianity, Vol. 2: Idealism and Christian Philosophy

To:
Hudson
Elliot
Nathanael
George

Acknowledgments

There are several friends and colleagues I would like to thank for their support in producing this little volume: Rob Caldwell, Josh Farris, Gerry McDermott, Ken Minkema, Jim Spiegel, Kyle Strobel, Tyler Taber, Seng Kong Tan, Greg Trickett and Jordan Wessling. I am particularly grateful to Mike McClymond and Graham Gould, both of whom offered me lengthy sets of thought-provoking questions, several of which I am still considering. I want to offer special thanks to Paul Helm and Doug Sweeney for their continuous encouragement, critical Edwardsian eye, and what is more, their interest in more than my mere academic success. I want to thank my doctoral supervisors, Oliver Crisp and Willem van Vlastuin, both of whom have been encouraging and insightful readers of my work. My wife has remained an immeasurable source of support throughout this project and so many others. Ten thousand acknowledgements could not possibly express my gratitude for her. It is to my four young sons, with their frequent quizzical stares (and rather surprising imaginative responses) at my attempts to explain to them some of Edwards' thinking about this otherwise exotic subject, that I dedicate this work. Finally, thank you to Rob Boss and *JESociety Press* for their interest in and enthusiasm for publishing this work.

SMH
Wells, ME
Summer 2017

Contents

Foreword	1
Introduction	5
Chapter 1– Spirits Are Real	17
Chapter 2– At the Fullness of Time	29
Chapter 3– Time and Causes	43
Chapter 4– Thirty Years a Man	59
Chapter 5– Jesus, Time and Causes	75
Conclusion	91
Bibliography	95

Foreword

It is difficult to avoid hard questions entirely, but it is much easier to avoid tackling hard questions when they are presented to us. Perhaps some of the hardest questions are theological in nature: "Why is there suffering in the world?"; "Is there a god?"; "For what can we hope?" These and many other existential questions cannot be avoided for they impress themselves upon us in the normal course of life. Nevertheless, we can avoid trying to answer them. Most people take this latter course when faced with hard questions. Few stop to look at them in detail, to stare unblinking at them, to try to fathom them. Fewer still, having faced such questions and found their answers wanting, stubbornly refuse to give up, preferring instead to continue the search for more adequate responses. The great New England pastor-theologian, Jonathan Edwards (1703–1758), was one of those rare human beings who, when faced with hard theological questions, refused to blink. He would not turn away and preoccupy himself with distractions that might help loosen the hold hard questions had upon his intellect. Instead, he made staring at these questions, and refusing to look away as he sought to find answers to them, the major scholarly preoccupation of his adult life.

These days, we may think such a person eccentric, or even somewhat unhinged. Why spend a lifetime doing that? But Edwards regarded this task as a vocation. As a young man, he wrote out a series of Resolutions, principles by which he sought to orient his life to the pole star of Divine Truth. In the first of these Resolutions, he wrote:

> Resolved, that I will do whatsoever I think to be most to God's glory, and my own good, profit and pleasure, in the whole of my duration, without any consideration of the time, whether now, or never so many myriads of ages hence. Resolved to do whatever I think to be my duty, and most for the good and advantage of mankind in general. Resolved to do this, whatever difficulties I meet with, how many and how great soever.

Such commitment led him to do extraordinary things. It also led him to extraordinary intellectual pursuits—for his was a life of the mind, first and foremost. Of these latter things much has been written. The scholarly world is now replete with works about various aspects of Edwards's thought and there is no sign of this interest abating. If anything, it grows with each passing year as more dissertations, monographs, essays, articles, and symposia roll off the presses. And, as one would expect with any sophisticated scholarly literature, how to understand Edwards on various points of detail has generated differing schools of interpretation.

In this work S. Mark Hamilton takes up some of the most distinctive, and most contested features of Edwards's thought. This has to do with a cluster of closely related and central themes in Edwards's work, namely, God, creation, and Christology. It is indicative of the quality of this work that its author manages to propose an important new way of thinking about these issues as they are presented to us in Edwards's literary remains. This is no mean feat. For not only do these issues represent some of the fundamental hard theological questions to which Edwards returned time and time again in his writings, but they mark him out as a superior thinker. They have also been subject to considerable critical scrutiny in the resurgence of interest in the scholarly work of Edwards that has flourished in the last half century.

Part of this reappraisal to which Hamilton treats his readers makes for uncomfortable reading for the present author—for his criticisms extend to my own work on Edwards. Yet what he says is a plausible alternative, and a genuine contribution to Edwardsian scholarship, which has given me pause for thought. That too is impressive. Not because my own interpretation of Edwards is superior or impregnable. (I for one am of the view that scholarly efforts are more often than not so much gossamer spun out over the course of our lives that are as fragile as the threads of a spider's web.) No, this aspect of Hamilton's essay is noteworthy because he gives even the seasoned Edwards scholar—such as the present author—pause for thought. Have I misunderstood? Has Hamilton got it right after all? Has he hit upon something that previous scholarship on these nodal questions has missed? It may be that Hamilton *is* right. He certainly presents his readers with a compelling interpretation of these matters in Edwards's work—matters at the heart of Edwardsian theology.

If, like Jonathan Edwards, you are perplexed by perplexing theological questions such as this little book tackles, then I encourage you like St Augustine to "take up and read!" For in Hamilton's short study you will find a work that clarifies and tests the coherence of the thought of one of the great intellects of the Christian tradition, shedding new light upon old (and hard) theological questions in the process.

Oliver D. Crisp
Fuller Theological Seminary
Pasadena, California

Introduction

The universe is created out of nothing every moment; and if it were not for our imaginations, which hinder us, we might see that wonderful work performed continually, which was seen by the morning stars when they sang together.

— Jonathan Edwards[1]

Few ideas in contemporary Christian theology are likely to invite as many quizzical stares as the so called doctrine of Continuous Creation. Surprisingly, there are several important theologians of the Protestant tradition for whom this doctrine has featured quite prominently, Jonathan Edwards arguably being the foremost. Continuous creation is, roughly, the idea that God's creating a particular thing *ex nihilo* (out of nothing), and his preservation of that thing are fundamentally the same timeless divine act.[2] In other words, God's

---

[1] Jonathan Edwards, *The Works of Jonathan Edwards*, Vol. 6, ed., Wallace E. Anderson (New Haven: Yale University Press, 1980), p. 241–42 (hereafter reference to the letterpress edition of the *Works of Jonathan Edwards* [vols. 1–26] shall appear as: *WJE*, followed by volume and page number; e.g.: *WJE* 6:241–42).

[2] For more on the contemporary interest in divine conservation, and the doctrine of continuous creation in particular, see: Alfred J. Freddoso, 'God's General Concurrence with Secondary Causes: Why Conservation is Not Enough' in James E. Tomberlin,

initial or original creative activity, though distinguishable as a primal divine act, is nevertheless indivisible from his subsequent sustaining or conserving activity.[3]

> ed., *Philosophical Perspectives 5*, (1991): 553-58, and 'Medieval Aristoteleanism and the Case against Secondary Causation in Nature' in Thomas V. Morris, (ed.) *Divine and Human Action, Essays in the Metaphysics of Theism* (Ithaca: Cornell University Press, 1988); Jonathan L. Kvanvig, and Hugh J. McCann, 'The Occasionalist Proselytizer: A Modified Catechism' in Tomberlin (ed.) *Philosophical Perspectives 5* (1991): 587:615; Hugh J. McCann, and Jonathan L. Kvanvig, 'Divine Conservation and the Persistence of the World' in Morris (ed.) *Divine and Human Action*; Andrew Pessin, 'Does Continuous Creation Entail Occasionalism? Malebranche (and Descartes)' in *Canadian Journal of Philosophy* 30 (2000): 413–40; Philip Quinn, 'Divine Conservation, Secondary Causes, and Occasionalism' in Morris (ed.) *Divine and Human Action*; and Steven Nadler, *Occasionalism: Causation Among the Cartesians* (Oxford: Oxford University Press, 2011).

[3] For an example of a stock-and-trade definition of divine conservation, one that Edwards was undoubtedly familiar with, consider William Ames (I am not the alone in referring to the relevance of Ames for our discussion of Edwards' doctrine of continuous creation; see: Seng Kong Tan, *Fullness Received and Returned: Trinity and Participation in Jonathan Edwards* [Minneapolis, MN: Fortress Press, 2014]). According to Ames, 'The providence of God is either *conservational or governmental*. Conservation is God's making all things, universal and particular, to persist and continue in *essence* and *existence* as well as in their powers, Ps. 104:19; Acts 17:28; Heb. 1:3. This is suitably called by the Schoolmen, "God's holding in his hand," because by this power God sustains all things as if with his hand. Conservation necessarily comes between creation and the government of things created, because whatever is created is for some end and use to which it ought to be directed and governed. But it cannot reach this end or be directed towards it, unless it be continued and maintained in its being *God's conservation is necessary for the creature because the creature depends in every way upon the creator—not only for its creation, but also for its being, existence, continuance, and operation*. Every creature would return to that state of nothing whence it came if God did not uphold it; and the cessation of divine conservation would, without any other operation, immediately reduce every creature to nothing. Some things—subject only to God—are conserved directly. *This conservation is the same as creation*, except that creation has a certain newness which conservation lacks and creation lacks a preceding existence which conservation implies. *Conservation is nothing else than a continued creation, so to speak, and therefore it is joined with creation*', William Ames, *The Marrow of Theology* ed. John Dykstra Eisden (Grand Rapids: Baker, 1968), 1.9.14–18, 108–9 (emphasis added). Interestingly, upon drawing the distinction between divine

INTRODUCTION

Far from being tucked away in the dark corners of Edwards' philosophical mind, his commitment to this curious doctrine is actually quite explicit. Accordingly, he argues that, 'God's preserving created things in being is perfectly equivalent to a *continuous creation*, or to his creating those things out of nothing at each moment of their existence'.[4] Elsewhere he explains that, '*All dependent existence whatsoever is in a constant flux, ever passing and returning; renewed every moment*, as the colours of bodies are every moment renewed by the light that shines upon them; and all is constantly proceeding from God, as light from the sun'.[5] In another place he argues that, '[E]very creature is

---

conservation and divine government, Ames makes a curious reference the doctrine of continuous creation. Notice the comprehensive way Ames describes God's post-creation activity. He conserves and governs his creation in four discernibly different ways: in 'being', in 'existence', in 'continuance', and in 'operation'. Now, we are left only to speculate about the precise meaning of these distinctions, as they are not something that Ames spells out any further. Perhaps Ames offers us something of a clue to his meaning when he describes 'some things—subject only to God—are conserved directly'. By 'some things' and 'directly' perhaps he means non-morally responsible agents; things which only require what he earlier describes as God's common (and not his 'special' or 'moral') government—things like the perpetual shifting desert sands of the Sahara or the seasonal appearance of Boston's radiant Autumn foliage or the annual growth rate of Redwoods in northern California's Muir Woods. He does, however, say 'every creature would return to a state of nothing', which seems to point in the direction of God's direct conservation of moral agents. It would be rather awkward, I think, to conceive of sands, leaves, and redwood trees as anything but created objects—certainly not creatures. In the end, we cannot be entirely sure of Ames' meaning. For what exactly in creation is not 'subject only to God'? For some further discussion of the nature of divine conservation in the post-reformation Reformed tradition, of which Ames was a central fixture, see e.g.: Francis Turretin, *Institutes of Elenctic Theology*, trans. George Musgrave Giger, ed. James Dennison Jnr. (Phillipsburg, NJ.: Presbyterian and Reformed, 1992–1997), 1.1., p. 489 (emphasis added); cf. Richard Muller, *Post Reformation Reformed Dogmatics: The Rise and Development of Reformed Orthodoxy, ca. 1520 to ca. 1725*, Vol. 3, The Divine Essence and Attributes (Grand Rapids. MI: Baker, 2003), pp. 384–92.

[4] *WJE* 3:401.

[5] *WJE* 3:404 (emphasis added).

every moment from God, and every moment created by him as much as the first moment; and that therefore the existence [of] the second moment is not individually the same with the existence [of] the first moment, *nor from it,* but *immediately from God*'.[6] In more than one place, Edwards goes so far as to explicitly attribute this creative work to God, the Son. For example, he writes,

> 'Tis evident that the same WORD, the same Son of God, that made the world or gave it being, also UPHOLDS it in being and governs it. This is evident in part unto reason. For upholding the world in being and creating of it, are not properly distinct works. For 'tis manifest that upholding the world in being is the same with a continued creation, and consequently that creating of the world is but the beginning of upholding of it, if I may so say, the beginning to give the world a supported and dependent existence; and preservation is only continuing to give it such a supported existence. So that truly the giving the world a being at first no more differs from preserving it through all successive moments, than the giving a being the last moment differs from the giving a supported being this moment.[7]

---

[6] '"Controversies" Notebook: Justification', *WJEO* 27 (emphasis added).

[7] "Miscellany", no. 1358, *WJE* 23:608. Edwards immediately afterwards gives his attention to an investigation of a series of additionally curious questions related to Trinitarian operations, including whether, 'if these things are so, what shall we think of the upholding and government of the world while Christ was in his humbled state? and while an infant, when he had less knowledge than afterwards, when it is said that he increased in wisdom and stature, and [had] far less strength than he had afterwards? when we are told that he was wearied with his journey, wearied and his strength in a measure spent only with governing the motions of his own body? Who upheld and governed the world at that time? Doubtless it will be said that God the

Now, to this point, some have claimed that statements such as these show that Edwards' version of continuous creation goes a step (others might say a leap) further than what I am calling a traditional account. More interesting still is that these supposed philosophical and theological excesses have led some interpreters to condemn Edwards' account as incoherent for its being fraught with an assortment of insuperable problems. The argument against Edwards has two broad parts and goes something like this.

According to the first part of the argument, on Edwards' account of God's continuous creation, created objects—what Edwards calls, 'all dependent existence'—persist through time for no more than a moment (however long that might be) before they cease to exist (some say, 'are destroyed'), whereupon facsimiles or copies of those created objects are then immediately re-created anew (ex nihilo), possessing all the necessary, incremental and perceptible changes that together generate the illusion of that created object's persistence through time.[8] And this occurs not only for mundane objects like chairs or bananas or airplanes but also for human beings (what Edwards calls 'created minds'), or so the argument goes. As a result, such interpreters argue—and this is where the real trouble begins—that on Edwards' view, continuously created humanity does not exist long enough—from one 'moment' to the next—to be responsible for any moral act, much less actually perform one.[9]

Father took the world out of the hands of the Son for that time, to uphold and govern it, and returned it into his hands again at his exaltation', p. 609.

[8] Oliver D. Crisp, *Jonathan Edwards and the Metaphysics of Sin* (Aldershort: Ashgate, 2003), p. 131 (hereafter, *JEMS*).

[9] Michael C. Rea, "The Metaphysics of Original Sin", in Peter van Inwagen and Dean Zimmerman, eds. *Persons: Human and Divine* (Oxford: Oxford University Press, 2007), pp. 319–56.

Part two of the argument says, interestingly, that when we consider this explanation of Edwards' doctrine of continuous creation in light of his account of Christ's humanity, its insuperable problems come to nought.[10] This is because of the eternal status of the Son and because he is the divine agent assigned with the performance of all moral acts attributed to the hypostatic union. In other words, because the causal activity of the Son is eternally 'constant' (a-temporal), it makes no difference whether his assumption of a created human nature is, as Edwards says, 'in constant flux'.[11]

It seems to me that there are several problems with both parts of this reasoning that beckon some further scrutiny. For, as I have argued elsewhere, Christ's human nature is for Edwards, 'the pattern of all'.[12] What this means, as we shall see, is that the same metaphysical apparatus that supports the being and activity (moral or otherwise) of the human nature of the God-man in the created world must also necessarily support the being and moral activity of all other human natures.[13] To this end, in the following five chapters, I argue for the

---

[10] Oliver D. Crisp, *Revisioning Christology: Theology in the Reformed Tradition* (Aldershot: Ashgate, 2011), pp. 43–67.

[11] It is interesting that Edwards' model of continuous creation is supposedly undermined by the fact that no human *person* exists long enough to perform a moral act, and yet according to an Orthodox, conciliar Christology, Jesus of Nazareth is not a human *person*, but has a human *nature*. This is a problem worth mentioning, and worth developing elsewhere.

[12] "Miscellany", no. 769, WJE 18:418; For discussion of the equivalent 'metaphysical apparatus' of Christ's humanity and humanity at large, see: S. Mark Hamilton, 'Jonathan Edwards, Hypostasis, Impeccability, and Immaterialism', *Neue Zeitschrift für Systematische Theologie und Religionsphilosophie* 58:2 (June 2016): 1–23.

[13] One notable difference between Edwards' Christological and his theological anthropology is that the source of Christ's humanity is (the Spirit of) the Father but for the rest of humanity it is (the Spirit of) the Son. Upon further exploration, this matter comes to the fore as a part of Edwards' so-called Spirit Christology.

coherence of both Edwards' doctrine of continuous creation as well as what I will refer to as Edwards' Continuous Christology.

Each of the following chapters is equal-parts philosophical clarification and theological construction. In chapters one through three, I attempt to recast several aspects of Edwards' ontology, a move that I go on to show in chapters four and five effectively recasts several aspects of Edwards' Christology. In the first chapter, I look closely at Edwards' commitment to a species of Immaterialism—roughly, the idea that all existence is mind-dependent. Or, to put it negatively, immaterialism is the idea that there is no material substance. In chapter two, I work out some of what Edwards thinks about the nature of time. Specifically, I offer up a slightly adjusted account of his commitment to what contemporary metaphysicians call Stage theory, which is a theory about how objects 'move' through or across time. Then, in chapter three, I direct my attention to Edwards' doctrine of Occasionalism, which is roughly idea that God is the sole causal agent in the universe, something I show does not undermine Edwards' preservation of human moral responsibility as it has been hitherto believed. Playing largely off the findings of the first chapter, in chapter four, I set out several aspects of Edwards' account of hypostasis, paying particular attention to what he says about the human nature of Jesus and the relationship that his humanity has to both the Son and humanity at large. Finally, in chapter five, I consider the Christological impact of Edwards' commitment to both stage theory and occasionalism. By way of conclusion, I offer up some suggestions for further research, specifically, those related to Edwards' Spirit Christology.

Now, this treatise being a piece of philosophical-theology, before we proceed, let me say a few things about its underlying method and, more specifically, explain what I mean by philosophical clarification and theological construction.

The Method

Methodologically speaking, this treatise is principally concerned in the first three chapters with what is sometimes called *philosophical clarification*.[14] By philosophical clarification, I mean, a method of exploring an idea (or set of ideas) or some proposition that possesses some inherently technical complexity, the bare meaning of which requires careful systematization and judicious explanation.[1]

Undertaking the philosophical clarification of Edwards' doctrine of continuous creation is something that has already been attempted by several philosophers and theologians, from which I have several important points of departure.[16] Philosophical clarification of Edwards' doctrine of continuous Christology has also appeared in one case,

---

[14] For a uniquely helpful treatment of *philosophical clarification*, see: Scott McDonald, 'What is Philosophical Theology?' In Kevin Timpe, ed., *Arguing About Religion* (New York & London: Taylor and Francis, 2009), p. 23.

[1] Such explorations, according to McDonald, are singularly 'concerned with understanding, developing, systematizing, and explaining [something]. It is possible to do all these things without raising the issue of its truth or justification for holding it. The fact is that a very large part of philosophy has nothing directly to do with the truth or justification of certain theories or propositions. The sort of conceptual analysis and systematic investigation I've described is the stuff of which philosophy is made, and philosophers would not know how to do their jobs if they could not do what our hypothetical moral realist is doing. Philosophers can, do, and must sometimes set aside questions of truth and justification in order to pursue these sorts of tasks', 'What is Philosophical Theology?', p. 24 (emphasis added).

[16] There have been number of brushes with Edwards' doctrine of continuous creation in the literature, including: Crisp, 'How Occasional was Jonathan Edwards' Occasionalism?' in Paul Helm and Oliver D. Crisp, *Jonathan Edwards: Philosophical Theologian* (Aldershot: Ashgate, 2003), pp. 61–76 (hereafter: *JEPT*). Stephen H. Daniel, 'Edwards' Occasionalism', in Don Schweitzer, ed. *Jonathan Edwards as Contemporary: Essays in Honor of Sang Hyun Lee* (New York, Peter Lang, 2010), pp. 1–14 (hereafter, *Jonathan Edwards as Contemporary*); Seng-Kong Tan, 'Trinitarian Action in the Incarnation' in *Jonathan Edwards as Contemporary*, pp. 127–50.

from which I will also dissent at several related points.[17] In both cases, discovering such clarity is a matter of determining whether what Edwards says is internally coherent. This is in contrast to a method of *philosophical justification* which has traditionally been concerned with establishing whether a particular belief (or set of beliefs) has evidential warrant and whether there is some resultant philosophical warrant for believing them.[18] Were this treatise concerned with a method of philosophical justification, we would concern ourselves primarily with determining whether Edwards' account of the God-world relation possesses sufficient (and in this case, Christologically-specific sufficient) philosophical grounds for our thinking it to be true and therefore believable. I am instead interested in bringing philosophical clarity to this Christologically-specific aspect of Edwards' philosophical-theology by determining whether what he says about the subject exhibits signs of coherence.

To this end my intent is as Scott McDonald describes, 'understanding, developing, systematizing, and explaining' what Edwards thinks about continuous creation as it relates in this particular case to the God-man—this is the theologically constructive part.[19] In other words, I intend to take the speculative step of determining what I think is the best explanation of what Edwards says about that which is material to his doctrine of continuous creation and fashioning a faithful account

---

[17] Crisp, *Revisioning Christology*, pp. 47–67.

[18] According to McDonald, 'Natural theology, whether strictly or broadly conceived, aims at discovering and providing acceptable epistemic support or grounding for theological truths. Strict and broad natural theology differ in their accounts of what constitutes acceptable epistemic support, but in either case the natural theologian is concerned with establishing the truth of certain theological propositions, thereby providing us with epistemic justification for and securing the rationality of our believing them. I will call this the concern for justifying theological truths', 'What is Philosophical Theology?', p. 23.

[19] McDonald, 'What is Philosophical Theology?', p. 24.

of what I take to be Edwards' commitment to an orthodox conciliar Christology.

Now, admittedly, Edwards does not make much of a public case for his doctrine of continuous creation, much less for his continuous Christology. That should not, however, prevent us from considering what he *might* have thought about such things in greater detail, a move for which there is considerable warrant. For Edwards published several important works in which appear some discussion of the doctrine, foremost of which appears in his *Great Doctrine of Original Sin Defended*. He also offered several (public) homilies which contain references to his continuous Christology. I take it therefore that his (however limited) public statements about these subjects were not insulated from his more private, academic thoughts about them. In other words, while we *don't* see evidence of his laboring at every turn to map his doctrine of continuous creation onto sermons about Christ from his Bridge Street pulpit, we do see evidence of him thinking about continuous creation in concert with various aspects of his theology from his Kings Street study.[20] How we measure the extent of

---

[20]That said, at least two homiletical exceptions appear during the later years of Edwards' Northampton tenure. For example, he argues on one occasion that, 'The great work of God in the application of redemption is singular and particular: a distinct work being wrought on every individual person. Though the work of God in the purchase of redemption be but one—all are included in one work—yet God's working this work on others [will be of no help] if there ben't a particular work of God's power and grace on their own hearts. Though [there be] never so many near relations [upon whom] God's almighty power is exerted, a new work of creation [must be enacted] on every heart, and this power must be continued [as] *a kind of continual creation*. God's act in justifying and accepting is particular, and God's work in glorifying is particular' ("Approaching the End of God's Grand Design", *WJE* 25:126 [emphasis added]). That Edwards never made all his thoughts public should not prevent us from considering how such a doctrinal relationship might have worked had he taken the time to work it out himself. What is of interest to me here is getting at and clarifying what Edwards might have actually thought—however private it may

his private philosophical and theological deliberations is one of the looming questions.

Arriving at a clear and coherent picture of Edwards' doctrine of continuous creation and the heavy metaphysical lifting it does for his Christology depends largely on our answers to other, more precise, questions like: *What*, exactly is continuously created? How long is an instant of time? Are there intervals between temporal instants? What is the relationship of one temporal instant to another? Is God the singular cause of all events that occur at a given temporal instant? What is a temporal stage? How many stages of time are there? And so on. So, with all this now in mind, let us now turn our attention to Edwards' account of continuous creation.

---

have been—about this aspect of his philosophical theology, despite his having not given explicit voice to it.

Chapter 1
Spirits Are Real

Those beings which have knowledge and consciousness are the only proper and real and substantial beings, inasmuch as the being of other things is only by these. From hence we may see the gross mistake of those who think material things the most substantial beings, and spirits more like a shadow; whereas spirits only are properly substance.

— Jonathan Edwards[1]

Introduction

CONTINUOUS CREATION IS a signal feature of Edwards' understanding of the God-world relationship. At a surprisingly early age, Edwards records in one of his private journals that 'Tis *certain* with me that the world exists anew every moment, that the existence of things every moment ceases and every moment is renewed'.[2] So apparently fixed in Edwards' thinking did the idea of God's continuous creation

---

[1] "Of Atoms", *WJE* 6:204, 207.

[2] "Miscellany", no. 125a, *WJE* 13:288 (emphasis added).

of the world become that he eventually affirmed it to be 'most agreeable to the Scripture, to suppose creation to be *performed new every moment*. The Scripture speaks of it not only as past but as a present, remaining, continual act. Job 9:9; Psalms 65:6, Psalms 104:4; Isaiah 40:22, Isaiah 44:24; Amos 5:8; and *very commonly* in the Scripture'.[3] God's continuous creation of the world is an idea that found expression at varying levels in Edwards' work throughout and until the very end of his life. At one point in a public sermon he makes the rather astonishing argument for what William Schweitzer aptly calls 'continuous redemption'.[4] Accordingly, Edwards writes,

---

[3] "Miscellany" no. 346, *WJE* 13:418 (emphasis added). For all the attempts to forge a genetic historical link between the Anglican Bishop and philosopher George Berkeley and Edwards, there are few so direct and similar links as their mutual discussion of creation-conservation and occasional causation. Rather startlingly, Berkeley argues (as does Edwards), 'For aught I can see, it is no disparagement to the perfection of God to say that all things necessarily dependent on Him as their Conservator as well as Creator, and that *all nature would shrink to nothing*, if not upheld and preserved in being by the same force that first created it. *This I am sure is agreeable to the Holy Scripture*, as well as to the writing of the most esteemed philosophers; and if it is to be considered that men make use of tools and machines to supply defect of power in themselves, we shall think it no honour to the Divinity to attribute such things to Him', *Philosophical Correspondence with Johnson*, 'II. Berkeley to Johnson [November 25, 1729]' in A.A. Luce and T.E. Jessop, eds. *The Works of George Berkeley Bishop of Cloyne* (New York: Thomas Nelson and Sons, 1949) 2:280–81 (emphasis added [hereafter, *WGB*]). Berkeley's argument assumes much of what I am intending to work out in this chapter, namely, that created minds (as Edwards call them) exist as substances in some real sense and do not, as Berekeley says 'shrink to nothing'. Sebastian Rehman has offered up a recent and most helpful article that retraces some of what has become a long history of efforts to show Berkeley's influence on Edwards in "Towards a Solution to the 'Perennially Intriguing Problem' of the Sources of Jonathan Edwards' Idealism", *Jonathan Edwards Studies* 5:2 (2015): pp.138–55 (hereafter 'Towards a Solution').

[4] William M. Schweitzer, *God is a Communicative Being: Divine Communicativeness and Harmony in the Theology of Jonathan Edwards* (New York: T&T Clark, Studies in Systematic Theology, 2012), p. 19.

> As God works grace so he establishes, confirms it and *continues to work* [grace] as the preservation of the world in being is a *continual creation* so is the preservation of grace in the heart. If God keeps men from falling from grace, if God should withdraw his *continued operation* Godly men would presently fall from Grace. Thus God works all that is wrought in the heart that is needful in order to salvation both before conversion, at conversion, in conversion and after conversion.[5]

Now, it may come as no surprise that Edwards leaves us without what we might call a full-orbed, systematic explanation of his thinking on the matter. In fact, in numerous places he assumes a great deal, metaphysically speaking, about the precise content of these claims, leaving his interpreters to the laborious and largely abductive work of hammering out what he actually thought. What we may nevertheless regard with a degree of minimum certainty is that for Edwards, the common systematic division of divine acts into 1) the initial creation of a thing and 2) the conservation (i.e., acts of Providence) of that thing means that he thinks that God's initial act of creation and his subsequent acts of conservation are somehow the same timeless act.

Achieving the clarity necessary to measure degrees of greater certainty about Edwards' thinking about continuous creation and, what is more, certainty about the implications that a commitment like continuous creation has for his Christology, requires that we first break down Edwards' doctrine of continuous creation into various, more manageable (though intimately related) constituents. The constituents that bear most significantly upon this doctrine are as I previously indicated, Edwards' immaterial realism, his four-dimensionalism, and his occasionalism. Now, it is not my intent to offer some

---

[5] *"Sermons, Series II, 1728–1729"*, n. 63, Hosea 13:9 (b), *WJEO* 43 (emphasis added).

thorough-going treatment of each of these subjects. My intent is rather to peel back, as it were, and examine in detail aspects of these intimately-related metaphysical layers of Edwards' thinking in order to then show how they bear upon his continuous Christology and the coherence of Edwards' doctrine of continuous creation at large. Let us begin with Edwards' immaterialism.

Created Minds (and their Bodies)

That Edwards conceives of created being in two categories—minds and ideas—is his immaterialism. To what species of immaterialism does Edwards subscribe—the *anti-realist* or the *realist* species?—is the next and more important question. To be an immaterialist *and* an anti-realist means (roughly) that while Edwards affirms the existence of created minds and ideas, he denies that created minds exist independently of the divine mind. In other words, created minds are not substances in their own right; God is the only true substance and created minds are radically dependent for their existence (and the existence of their ideas) upon the divine mind.[6] This has become the majority interpretation of Edwards' immaterialism in recent years.[7]

---

[6] It is interesting that some interpreters argue with confidence that Edwards is an *anti-realist*, although they also admit of the fact that Edwards at times—more times than perhaps they would like to admit—can be coherently read along a realist line. For example, according to Oliver Crisp, one could make the case for Edwards being an immaterial *realist*. With some admittedly disparate, but still notable, support from Edwards, Crisp argues that 'one could make metaphysical room, as it were, for the existence of minds that were not necessarily radically dependent on God or their continued existence, i.e. were not dependent for their continued existence on God continuing to think of them', *Revisioning Christology*, p. 53.

[7] See e.g.: Joshua R. Farris and S. Mark Hamilton, eds. *Idealism and Christianity: Idealism and Christian Theology*, vol. 1, (New York: Bloomsbury, 2016).

For Edwards to be classified as a realist could mean a number of things, especially in contemporary philosophical terms. For the purpose of exploring his doctrine of continuous creation, and his continuous Christology in turn, it has primarily to do with two things: 1) the ontological status of created minds—whether and how they exist independent of other minds (particularly, the divine mind)—and 2) whether or not Edwards regards created minds at all as substances. Indeed, the answer to both of the questions bear significantly on whether Edwards' thinking on these matters of God's continuously creative activity is coherent or not.

Regarding the later claim, it is my contention that Edwards thought created minds were indeed substances; *substantialized* by virtue of their peculiar relationship to the Son's human nature. Regarding the former claim, I maintain that the created mind of Jesus of Nazareth is as all other created minds: at one level, no less radically dependent on the divine mind for its existence and nevertheless *not* contingent for its existence upon the perception of any other created mind. In these ways, the human nature of the God-man is, as it were, the pattern or archetype for created minds. Dissenting from what is arguably the majority report of Edwards' metaphysics, with what remains of this chapter, I offer up some additional philosophical clarification for what it means for Edwards to be committed to immaterial *realism*.

Realism and Created-Mind-Independence

Edwards very flatly says that, 'The substance of bodies at last comes to nothing, or nothing but the Deity acting in that particular manner in those parts of space where he thinks fit. So that, speaking most strictly, *there is no proper substance but God himself*.[8] Prima facie, this

---

[8] "Of Atoms" *WJE* 6:215.

does not exactly bode well for the ensuing argument. For, if God is the only 'proper substance' it seems, as others contend, that Edwards made no room in his ontology for substances of any other sort. Right? There are several statements like this one in Edwards' philosophical writings that have funded what has become something of a consensus in the literature, namely, that Edwards was committed to some sort of metaphysical *anti-realism*, according to which, all that exists outside of the mind of God is somehow radically dependent upon God's immediate thinking of them for their continued existence. Or to put it simply, this is the idea that Edwards believed there to be no mind-independent existence.

It is interesting, however, that Edwards also says things like, '*beings* which have knowledge and consciousness are the only proper and real and substantial beings [because] *spirits* are the only proper substance'.[9] And elsewhere he says, 'those beings which have knowledge and consciousness are the only proper and *real* and *substantial* beings, inasmuch as the being of other things is only by these. From hence we may see the gross mistake of those who think material things the most substantial beings, and spirits more like a shadow; whereas *spirits only are properly substance*'.[10] This is quite different than the statement in the previous paragraph, one with which Edwards seems, at first glance, to be contradicting himself. For we can only assume that, at least in this instance, by 'spirits' he means both uncreated and created 'spirits' or minds alike (similar again to Bishop George Berkeley, Edwards often employs the terms 'spirit' and 'mind' interchangeably[11]).

---

[9] "Of Being", *WJE* 6:206 (emphasis added).

[10] "Of Atoms", *WJE* 6:204, 207.

[11] For some helpful discussion of 'Berkeleyan Spirits', see John Russell Roberts' seminal work: *Metaphysics for the Mob: The Philosophy of George Berkeley* (Oxford: Oxford University Press, 2007).

But there is more. Edwards argues similarly 'when I say, "the material universe exists only in mind", I mean that it is absolutely dependent on the conception of the mind for its existence, and does not exist as spirits do, whose existence does not consist in, nor in dependence on, the conception of other minds'.[12] Here he goes a step further, differentiating between the existence of 'spirits', who (he appears to think) exist independent of mind or thought, and the universe, that exists as both complex sets and simple ideas in the mind. Thus, I take it that Edwards thinks that ideas and minds somehow exist quite differently from one another. The question of interest for us then is, *how* they exist differently.

The following statement offers quite a telling answer to this question. Edwards explains 'things as to God exist from all eternity alike. That is, the idea is always the same, and after the same mode. *The existence of things, therefore, that are not actually created minds, consists only in power,* or in the determination of God that such and such ideas shall be raised in created minds upon such conditions'.[13] Categorically speaking, the only things that are 'not actually created minds' are, on Edwards' ontology, ideas. A created mind, then, has the idea of a thing only insofar as that idea—whether simple or complex—is communicated to their minds by God through their senses.[14] Notice how Edwards differentiates between the existence of created minds

---

[12] "The Mind", *WJE* 6:368.

[13] "The Mind", n. 35, *WJE* 6:355 (emphasis added).

[14] It is interesting that Edwards distinguishes between complex and simple ideas in terms of 'substances' and what he calls 'modes'. He argues, 'the distribution of the objects of our thoughts into substances and modes may be proper, if by substance we understand a complexion of such ideas which we conceive of as subsisting together and by themselves; and by modes, those simple ideas which cannot be themselves, or subsist in our mind alone', "The Mind", *WJE* 6:350 (According to Anderson, Edwards' distinction of complex and simple ideas and their attached meanings follows the Cartesianism reflected in Arnauld's, *Art of Thinking*; see: *WJE* 6:350, n. 3).

and things that 'consist only in power' and notice that he calls those things that consist only in power, 'ideas' (he says the same thing when he talks about 'continuous redemption'[15]). The implication here is that when Edwards offers up his famous defense for the doctrine of Original Sin, for instance, saying that 'all dependent existence whatsoever is *in a constant flux, ever passing and returning; renewed every moment, as the colours of bodies are every moment renewed by the light that shines upon them; and all is constantly proceeding from God, as light from the sun*', what I think he means by 'all dependent existence' is strictly speaking, that which is perceptible to created minds, *not* created minds themselves.[16] This is a not inconsiderable shift in how we make sense of Edwards' immaterialism. To put it differently, 'all dependent existence' for a created mind is that which is ideal; what is 're-newed every moment' are ideas or percepts, *not* created minds. Minds have a moment-to-moment existence that is quite different than ideas. Minds seem to endure while ideas or percepts seem to perdure or exdure (about which, more in a moment). The sun is itself not renewed every moment, to borrow Edwards' oft-cited analogy. Rather, it is the beams of the sun's light (and in one sense, the physical human eyes that see them) that are renewed every moment. So when it comes to Edwards' account of continuous creation, what is

---

[15] See: Schweitzer, *God is a Communicative Being*, p. 19.

[16] WJE 3:404 (emphasis added). Edwards remarks similarly elsewhere that, 'Since, as has been shewn, body is nothing but an infinite resistance in some part of space caused by the immediate exercise of divine power, it follows that as great and as wonderful a power is every moment exerted to the upholding of the world, as at first was to the creation of it; the first creation being only the first exertion of this power to cause such resistance, the preservation only the continuation or the repetition of this power every moment to cause this resistance. So that *the universe is created out of nothing every moment*; and *if it were not for our imaginations, which hinder us, we might see that wonderful work performed continually, which was seen by the morning stars when they sang together*', WJE 6:241–42.

being continuously created, it appears from this, are merely ideas, *not* minds.

Consider how Edwards explains this divine action in some more refined detail, when he argues that '[God] causes all changes to arise as if all these things had actually existed in such a series in some created mind, and as if created minds had comprehended all things perfectly'.[17] Notice again that Edwards is not saying that created minds are changed or re-newed, but only the minds' perceptions. What this means is that when we read statements where Edwards seems to equate the mind-dependent status of bodies *and* spirits as anti-real—statements like: '[W]hat we call body is nothing but a particular mode of perception; and what we call spirit is nothing but a composition and series of perceptions, or a universe of coexisting and successive perceptions connected by such wonderful methods and laws'—I think we need to be more discriminating of what I will henceforth refer to as Edwards' *relative realism*. By relative realism I mean the difference between *created-mind-indepedence* and *uncreated-mind-indepedence*.[18] This is an important distinction for making sense of Edwards' idealism in general, but in particular, as we will see in the next stage of the chapter, for his account of the nature of the man, Jesus of Nazareth.

Now, generally speaking, something is real if that something has mind-independent existence. What I am calling *relative realism* describes something that is *created*-mind-independent, that is, some-

---

[17] "The Mind", WJE 6:354.

[18] "Notes on Knowledge and Existence", WJE 6:398 See also: 'The existence and motion of every atom has influence, more or less, on a motion of all other bodies in the universe, great or small, as is most demonstrable from the laws of gravity. God's constitution that some of our ideas shall be connected with others according to such a settle law and order, so that some ideas shall follow from others as their cause', "The Mind", WJE 6:358. (Compare with: "The Mind," n. 13, WJE 6:344).

thing which is not contingent on a *created* minds' perception of it, namely, other created minds.[19] In other words, just because something may be radically dependent for its existence on the uncreated (divine) mind, it does not necessarily follow that it has no independent existence from created minds. This is a subtle, but crucial refinement for our making sense of both Edwards' doctrine of continuous creation and his continuous Christology. To reiterate, all things are in some sense mind-dependent insofar as those things are dependent upon the uncreated mind of God, who *is* mind or *is* a mind or *has* a mind. Relative realism, by contrast, refers to the way things exist (including other minds) in created minds alone. For Edwards' part, it appears that those objects which are *real* are reducible to nothing less than two things: created minds and laws of nature (we will consider laws of nature in more detail in the section on occasionalism). What this means for understanding Edwards' immaterialism is that God is really the sole cause of moment-to-moment continuously created percepts. A human body then, is for Edwards not only a strictly physical phenomenon. It is a complex idea in the divine mind that is immediately and continuously communicated anew (i.e., every moment) to perceiving (created) minds, including, as we shall see in a moment, the created mind of Jesus of Nazareth.[20] It is by making this distinction that we can see how Edwards can conclude an extended discussion in his notebook, "Of Being", on the uncreated-mind-dependence of all things in the absence of a created-minds perceptions, saying, 'there

---

[19] I am grateful to Greg Trickett who pointed out a similar distinction in Berkeley's idealism, about which he wrote in some detail in his "Realist Conception of Truth", in James S. Spiegel and Steve Cowan, eds., *Idealism and Christianity: Idealism and Christian Philosophy*, Vol. 2 (New York: Bloomsbury Academic, 2016), pp. 29–50.

[20] "The Mind," entry n. 62, *WJE* 6:377–80 (Edwards calls things like gravity and laws of nature, 'shadows of excellency', a category often curiously attributed to his descriptions of the divine).

is nothing in a room shut up, but only in God's consciousness. How can anything be there any other way?' and yet go on to say in the same entry that

> It follows from hence, that *those beings* which have knowledge and consciousness are the only proper and *real* and *substantial* beings, inasmuch as the being of other things is only by these. From hence we may see the gross mistake of those who think material things the most substantial beings, and spirits more like a shadow; whereas *spirits only are properly substance.*[21]

Given what I am calling *relative realism,* the evidence here seems to suggest that Edwards thinks created minds are indeed real and therefore substances of some sort in their own right, however reduced or derivative they might be. The next question for us to consider is: In what way are they derivative? Because part of the answer to this question is thoroughly Christological, the manner in which created minds are substances is something to which I will return when discussing Edwards' continuous Christology in chapters 4 and 5; we must work out some of the metaphysics of Edwards' doctrine of continuous creation first, before we consider any detailed discussion of the metaphysics of his continuous Christology. Let us therefore turn to second part of this Edwardsian puzzle, namely, his commitment to four-dimensionalism and more specifically, *Stage Theory.*

---

[21]"Of Atoms", *WJE* 6:204, 207.

CHAPTER 2

AT THE FULLNESS OF TIME

[God] causes all changes to arise as if all these things had actually existed in such a series in some created mind, and as if created minds had comprehended all things perfectly.

— Jonathan Edwards[1]

Introduction

YOU MIGHT BE THINKING, 'What could the nature of time possibly have to do with Christology'?! The simple answer is, a lot, actually.[2] That the nature of time is a factor for understanding our doctrine should actually be less surprising than it is in contemporary theology. The Scriptures are replete with talk of time, from which a great deal is often assumed (and perhaps mistakenly) about how we

---

[1] "The Mind", *WJE* 6:354 (emphasis added).

[2] For a fascinating essay about the nature of time and the doctrine of salvation, see: Ryan Mullins, 'Identity Through Time and Personal Salvation' in Marc Cortez, Joshua R. Farris, and S. Mark Hamilton, eds., *Being Saved: Explorations in Constructive Soteriology* (London: SCM Press, forthcoming 2018).

think time actually works and what is more, how we think objects move through it, so to speak, from this moment to that.[3]

In contemporary philosophical terms, Edwards is, as we shall see, reliably regarded as an *eternalist*. Eternalists (generally) think that objects are carved up in terms of temporal and spatial parts of some sort, thereby giving non-present objects a real and present status. This is in contrast to the *presentist*, who thinks that nothing exists, save for that which exists now, at this moment. Now, if we take the eternalist distinction a step further in our understanding of Edwards, we arrive at another, more careful categorization of his thought, namely, *Four-dimensionalism*.[4] Four-dimensionalism is the idea that ordinary objects like cupcakes, candles, and clouds persist through time somewhat similar to how they extend through space.[5]

There are two basic questions about Edwards' four-dimensionalism—and his more refined commitment to *Stage theory* in particular—that bear upon the ensuing discussion.[6] The first has to do with

---

[3] See e.g.: Genesis 1:1; Psalm 90:2, 10; Psalm 139:14. Matthew 13:39, 18:26, 24:35, 25:10; Mark 10:6; Luke 24:27, 44; John 6:39–40, 44, 54, 12:48; 1 Corinthians 4:18, 15:23–24, 26; Ephesians 1:9–10; Galatians 4:4; Hebrews 1:11, 9:1–10; 2 Peter 3:10–11; Hebrews 9:27; 1 Timothy 4:2; 1 Timothy 2:6; Revelation 7:16–17, 20:3, 21:1, 4.

[4] For some additional discussion of Edwards' commitment to stage theory, see: S. Mark Hamtlon, "Jonathan Edwards on the Election of Christ", *Neue Zeitschrift für Systematische Theologie und Religionsphilosophie* 58:6 (December 2016): 1–25.

[5] There are a number of Four-Dimensionalist ontologies, such as, growing-block theory, shrinking-tree theory, and stage theory. For some helpful clarification of these various theories, see: Michael Rea, "Four-Dimensionalism", in Michael J. Loux and Dean W. Zimmerman, eds. *The Oxford Handbook of Metaphysics*, (New York: Oxford University, 2003), pp. 246–80.

[6] Building upon anti-realist assumptions about Edwards immaterialism, Oliver Crisp provides a subtly different account Edwards' stage theory, saying, 'The world comprises all created minds and their ideas, which exist 'in' God. 'Matter' is a fiction; there are no material objects strictly speaking, though there are objects that have properties such as 'being hard', 'being extended in space', etc. But these are no more

what I will call 'stage-content', by which I mean, the various constituents or composite structure of particular stages. The second, and intimately related aspect, has to do with what I will call 'stage-intervals' and how one stage 'fits' together with another. I've chosen these two terms purposively in order to avoid what is a veritable black hole of a discussion about the nature of time that could quite easily steer our particular interests off course. These categories will, I think, make our discussion of Edwards' four-dimensionalism much more navigable. The intent of the ensuing discussion is concerned with showing that Edwards' account of temporal persistence hangs on his commitment to immaterial realism without which his commitment to either continuous creation or a continuous Christology would indeed be incoherent. More to the point, I am concerned with subtly augmenting the way we look at how Edwards conceives of temporal stages, namely, by showing that temporal stages are in fact composed merely of percepts or ideas, not minds.

---

than sensations, percepts, ideas – there is nothing over and above such ideal entities that must be taken account of in metaphysics. The world exists in God as a set of stable ideas. But the world is not an entity that persists through time upon being created by God. Rather, God creates a four-dimensional set of numerically distinct world-stages that exist across time, and that he segues together seriatim, according to his good pleasure and will. *This means that the world is created whereupon it immediately ceases to exist*, to be replaced by a second momentary facsimile world created *ex nihilo*. *This too immediately ceases to exist* and replaced by another facsimile … and so on, each world-stage being succeeded by another seriatim, in the divine mind. Thus the 'world' (i.e. the created order as it exists across space and time) is in reality a collection of world-stages. What is more, God causes these world-stages to obtain in the sequence they do, giving them the appearance of continuity through apparently stable laws and principles of operation. But God is the sole cause of the obtaining of these world-stages as well as being the causal agent responsible for all that obtains in these world stages. Creatures are merely the occasions of God's action'; Crisp, "On the Orthodoxy of Jonathan Edwards", *Scottish Journal of Theology* 67.3 (2014): 304–22.

Stage Theory

Stage theorists think that created objects are divisible into spatial and temporal 'stages' rather than, as some had supposed to this point, spatial and temporal 'parts'.[7] The technical difference between persistence as 'stages' and persistence as 'parts' amounts to a distinction between an individuated time and space slices of a thing versus a thing that has, as the stage theorist argues, temporal and spatial *counterparts*.[8] To work out this difference with more clarity, consider a mundane example of a chocolate cupcake—Edwards had a great affinity for chocolate.[9]

On Edwards' way of thinking about persistence, a chocolate cupcake has various spatial parts—parts of the cupcake that occupy distinct spatial regions, like the chocolate icing-part, the sprinkles-part, and the cake-part, et cetera. None of these parts are numerically identical nor do they occupy the same spatial region (strictly speaking, the sprinkles are only on top of the icing-part, which is on top of the cake-part), even though together they occupy the same spatial region called 'a chocolate cupcake'. Such objects not only have spatial parts, on Edwards' view, they also have temporal parts, like the cupcake-in the oven, the cupcake-cooling on the counter, the cupcake-in Edwards'

---

[7] The distinction between Edwards' four-dimensionalism being described as a temporal parts and now temporal stages theory is a recent development. For a work that is reflective of this subtle interpretive revision, see: Crisp, "On the Orthodoxy of Jonathan Edwards", pp. 304–22.

[8] For a detailed argument for of Stage theory, see: Katherine Hawley, *How Things Persist* (Oxford: Oxford University, 2001), pp. 189–91. For a more recent and additionally helpful, though brief account of Stage theory, see: Bradford Skow, *Objective Becoming* (Oxford: Oxford University Press, 2015), pp. 216–21.

[9] See: George Marsden, *Jonathan Edwards: A Life* (New Haven: Yale University Press, 2004) p. 420.

mouth, the cupcake-digesting in Edwards' large intestine, and so on and so forth.

Strictly speaking, however, these cupcake-stages exist at different times on analogy with the physical parts that populate those stages of an object at any given moment. What this means is that when we talk about the cupcake-cooling on the counter, we are really talking about a cupcake-stage, of which there are various (perhaps infinite numbers of) cupcake-stage-counterparts, depending on the duration of the cupcake's station on the counter (and whether time is construed as *discrete* or *dense*—about which, more in a moment).[10] This, again, is ever-so-subtly distinguishable from what is often called a *Temporal Parts* theory, according to which objects, like cupcakes, persist through time as numerically distinct parts of a single spatiotemporally extended object that is ever only partly present at each time and space index that it occupies.[11]

On the temporal parts model, we cannot truly be talking about the cupcake unless we are talking about the aggregate or sum of all the cupcake's spatial and temporal parts, together which form the idea of the cupcake. Temporal parts-references to Edwards' cupcake then are technically speaking, references *only* to cupcake-parts. Stage theory-references to cupcakes, however, are references to the whole cupcake at a particular temporal interval. At this point, you must be asking, 'so, what then do counterpart cupcakes have to do with continuous creation and continuous Christology'?

In terms of continuous creation, a temporal-parts understanding of Edwards' chocolate cupcake says that what God brings into

---

[10] Hawley, *How Things Persist*, p. 51.

[11] Rea, "Four Dimensionalism", in *Oxford Handbook to Metaphysics*, p. 246. This view is sharply distinct from Endurantism, which explains that objects persist through time by their being altogether present at each moment they exist.

existence each moment are numerically distinct temporal and spatial cupcake-parts across the duration of the cupcake's existence.[12] The continued existence of the cupcake parts are thereby a continuously creative divine act—each temporal and spatial part of the cupcake is immediately created out of nothing and renewed with each successive moment; each moment containing only part of the whole cupcake. Again, this is because the cupcake, as the temporal part theorist sees it, is strictly speaking, *never all there*. And here is the subtle, but altogether important difference. According to the stage theorists' reading of Edwards' cupcake, what God is continuously creating are counterpart or facsimile chocolate cupcakes. In this way, the cupcake *is all there* (momentarily) at whatever determined temporal and spatial slice of time it exists (or is 'published', to borrow a term from Berkeley).[13] This difference between a time slice that is a temporal (and spatial) *part* of a thing versus a time slice that is a temporal (and spatial) *counterpart* makes a significant difference for how we arrive a coherent picture of Edwards' doctrine of continuous creation of mundane things, but more importantly for his continuous creation of created minds and the mind of Jesus of Nazareth in particular. Determining this difference is a matter of understanding further what I earlier referred to as 'stage-content'.

---

[12] According to Rea, an object's temporal parts, 'are like spatially distant objects: they exist, just not here, where we are', Ibid., p. 246. The implication for Edwards' chocolate cupcake is that there is a potentially indeterminate and duration-less number of temporal and spatial cupcake stages that might be conceived.

[13] I am conscious that an A-theorist about time might object to the claim that a temporal stage of a thing means that that thing is in any which way 'all there' at a given moment. By 'all there', I am not saying that each stage of a thing is numerically identical with the others. Any account of an objects change on a B-theory of time, especially one as exotic as Stage theory, would seem to block such a claim. By 'all there' I am only trying to distinguish between the way a temporal parts theorist thinks about objects and tensed time and the way a stage theorist thinks about it.

'Stage-Content', Created Minds, and Percepts

When we talk about what I am calling 'stage-content', we are attempting to isolate or distinguish the various properties of a particular stage, one from another; not stages, one from another, but the collective elements of a single, individuated counterpart stage or slice of time. Imagine for a moment that we were somehow able to slow time down like a film editor does to a film, so that we are able to watch it according to frame by frame progress—a move similar to the one that Edwards ironically seems to think would establish the truth of continuous creation—so we might examine the composite structure of one frame (i.e., stage) in particular.[14] By examining the stage-counterpart structure in this way, I am offering up slight revision to the majority report on Edwards' stage theory in the literature, which has to this point been underpinned by anti-realist assumptions about Edwards' immaterialism and is as a result much the cause for the charge of incoherence leveled against his doctrine of continuous creation. Or to put it differently, I think revising Edwards' stage theory to account for his immaterial realist commitment is a key to establishing the coherence of both Edwards' doctrine of continuous creation in general and his continuous Christology in particular.

The signal difference between an anti-realist understanding of a temporal stage and its relationship to other temporal stages and a realist understanding of a temporal stage and its related stages hinges on the difference between the relation of minds and ideas to those stages. And the difference is this. I think that the content of these temporal stages is made up of various simple and complex

---

[14] 'The universe is created out of nothing every moment; and if it were not for our imaginations, which hinder us, we might see that wonderful work performed continually, which was seen by the morning stars when ...they sang together.' *WJE* 6:241–42.

ideas, which together compose stages that are *nothing more than mental projections; divine mental projections*, to be more precise.

This way of looking at the relationship of temporal stages is like looking at a series of blank canvases or canvas-stages on which are painted various perceptible images that created minds perceive at different times, of which they are only an ideal (self-perceived) part. In other words, created minds stand apart from or above these stages, as it were, in order to perceive them; even to the point of their perceiving their own participation in each canvas-stage scenario. This is what writers sometimes call writing from the 'omniscient perspective', that is, from the imaginative perspective of, say, an alternate person or inanimate object in a given story. And herein lies the critical distinction at issue for the coherence of Edwards' account of conservation: the content of stages that are continuously created, including the ones for Jesus of Nazareth are purely ideal. That is, to keep the analogy going, created minds are never painted into the picture in the same way their ideas are.

The difference here, in more technical terms, is that Edwards thinks that created minds endure across temporal stages, while ideas *exdure* across them. This language is both technical and a bit tricky. To endure across time is generally associated with presentist assumptions about persistence whereas to exdure across time is almost exclusively attributed to eternalist and in particular, stage theorist assumptions about persistence. To say that created minds endure is to say that they are constants while to that say ideas exdure is to say that they—whether complex or simple—are divisible into intervals of percepts. Minds are only ever observing, even though images of themselves (images of their bodies, actually) are somehow a part of these canvas-stages. This is because minds, harkening back to our previous discussion about created-mind-independence, are (indivisible) and simple substances while ideas are not. This is why when

Edwards says things like, '[God] causes all changes to arise *as if* all these things had actually existed in such a series in some created mind, and as if created minds had comprehended all things perfectly', he does not say that *created minds* exist in a series of moments.[15] This is because, similar to the uncreated mind God, Edwards seems to think that created minds exist independently of those stage-percepts.[16]

---

[15] "The Mind", *WJE* 6:354.

[16] Edwards undertakes several protracted discussions about the status of uncreated ideas and minds that help us understand the shape of his thinking. At one point, and here I quote him at length, he writes, 'Since all material existence is only idea, this question may be asked: In what sense may those things be said to exist which are supposed, and yet are in no actual idea of any created minds? I answer, they exist only in uncreated idea. But how do they exist otherwise than they did from all eternity, for they always were in uncreated idea and divine appointment? I answer, they did exist from all eternity in uncreated idea, as did everything else and as they do at present, but not in created idea. But, it may be asked, how do those things exist which have an actual existence, but of which no created mind is conscious—for instance the furniture of this room when we are absent and the room is shut up and no created mind perceives it—how do these things exist? I answer, there has been in times past such a course and succession of existences that these things must be supposed to make the series complete, according to divine appointment of the order of things; and there will be innumerable things consequential which will be out of joint—out of their constituted series—without the supposition of these. For upon supposition of these things are infinite numbers of things otherwise than they would be, if these were not by God thus supposed; yea, the whole universe would be otherwise, such an influence have these things by their attraction and otherwise. Yea, there must be an universal attraction in the whole system of things from the beginning of the world to the end; and to speak more strictly and metaphysically we must say, in the whole system and series of ideas in all created minds, so that these things must necessarily be put in to make complete the system of the ideal world. That is, they must be supposed if the train of ideas be in the order and course settled by the supreme mind. So that we may answer in short, that the existence of these things is in God's supposing of them, in order to the rendering complete the series of things—to speak more strictly, the series of ideas—according to his own settled order and that harmony of things which he has appointed. The supposition of God which we speak of is nothing else but God's acting in the course and *series of his exciting ideas*, as if they, the things supposed, were in actual idea', "The Mind", *WJE* 6:357.

Imagine that you are actually watching Monet paint his famed *Waterlilies*. With the various canvas arranged in a lineal series of canvas-stages, Monet moves from one canvas to the next, painting his masterpiece. Monet in this analogy is of course, God, having the perfect idea of his masterpiece in full mental view (across the canvas-stages).[17] An echo of this analogy can be heard when Edwards says things like,

> 'Tis [the] perfection of God's idea that makes all things truly and properly present to him from all eternity, and is the reason why God has no succession. For everything that is, has been, or shall be, having been perfectly in God's idea *from all eternity*, and a perfect idea (which yet no finite being can have of anything) being the very thing; therefore, all things from eternity were equally present with God, and there is no alteration made in [his] idea by presence and absence *as there is in us*.[18]

Now imagine that Monet arranges his canvases to sit atop a series of subtly-backward-leaning easels, at a certain, fixed and optimal

---

[17] In Miscellany 94, Edwards argues 'I am satisfied that though this word "begotten" had never been used in Scripture, it would have been used in this case: there is no other word that so properly expresses it. 'Tis this perfection of God's idea that makes all things truly and properly present to him from all eternity, and is the reason why God has no succession. For everything that is, has been, or shall be, having been perfectly in God's idea from all eternity, and a perfect idea (which yet no finite being can have of anything) being the very thing; therefore, all things from eternity were equally present with God, and there is no alteration made in [his] idea by presence and absence as there is in us', *WJE* 13:258.

[18] "Miscellany" no. 94, *WJE* 13:258. Compare with, 'Things as to God exist from all eternity alike. That is, the idea is always the same, and after the same mode. The existence of things, therefore, that are not actually in created minds consists only in power, or in the determination of God that such and such ideas shall be raised in created minds upon such conditions', "The Mind", *WJE* 6:355.

height, each one illumined by a certain, fixed and optimal light. The canvases, of course, represent the temporal status and duration of God's moment-to-moment creation of all perceptions; each canvas-stage governed by various settled or fixed and established laws of nature, like gravity, for example. Canvases in this case are merely ideas that we are presented with every moment whereas the laws of nature, like gravity, are in fact real. Again there is an echo of this analogy in Edwards when he explains that 'the existence and motion of every atom has influence, more or less, on a motion of all other *bodies* in the universe, great or small, as is most demonstrable from the laws of gravity'.[19] Here are Edwards' canvas-stages. Elsewhere Edwards defends the idea that

> God supposes [a things'] existence; that is, he causes all changes to arise as if all these things had actually existed in such a series in some created mind, and as if created minds had comprehended all things perfectly. And although created minds do not, yet the divine mind doth, and he orders all things according to his mind, and his ideas.[20]

Accordingly, to keep the analogy going, you watch in wonder as Monet-canvas-stage by canvas-stage-steadily brings his masterpiece into your full view.[21] It is this sort of construction that I think Edwards

---

[19] "The Mind", *WJE* 6:358. Compare with: 'God's constitution that some of our ideas shall be connected with others according to such a settle law and order, so that some ideas shall follow from others as their cause', "The Mind", *WJE* 6:359. This is also a clue into how we ought to understand the function of Edwards' doctrine of occasionalism, namely, that divine causes are limited to perceptions (more in a moment).

[20] "The Mind," no. 34, *WJE* 6:354 (emphasis added).

[21] I am not necessarily hereby suggesting that Edwards thought created minds exist in an a-temporal parallel stage like some sort of hypertime. It is not entirely clear

has in mind—time and space being series' of canvases on which God continuously paints his perceptible masterpieces and created minds stand next to God, as it were, observing it all, including those projections of themselves. Edwards says at one point,

> The secret lies here: that which is truly the substance of *all bodies* is the infinitely exact and precise and perfectly stable idea in God's mind, together with his stable will that the same shall be *gradually communicated* to us, and to other minds, according to certain fixed and exact established methods and laws. The infinitely exact and precise divine idea, together with an answerable, perfectly exact, precise and stable will with respect to correspondent communications to created minds, and effects on their minds.[22]

Notice briefly, Edwards' classification of bodies as 'ideas' which are 'gradually communicated' and dependent upon 'fixed laws' for their being properly communicated to created minds. It is for this reason that I think Edwards understands created minds as existing in some sense apart from the percept-stages they occupy, kind of like how an actor acts in a film (to change the analogy) and then views himself acting in that film at the film's theater debut. But what about Edwards'

---

to me how Edwards conceives of the state in which created minds relate to the stages they 'occupy'. For a recent defense and compelling account of hypertime, see: Hud Hudson, *The Fall and Hypertime* (Oxford: Oxford University Press, 2014). Perhaps, taking a cue from Sebastian Rehnman's account of Edwards' immaterialism, Edwards thinks in way as does Descartes, namely, that Minds exist only in time but are independent of space (by virtue of their being without spatial extension, see: Rene Descartes, "Third Meditation" in *Meditations on First Philosophy*, trans. Donald A. Cress (Indianapolis, IN: Hackett Publishing, 1993).

[22] "The Mind", n. 13, *WJE* 6:344 (emphasis added).

understanding of 'fixed laws'? What are those? In order to complete our augmented account of Edwards' stage theory, and answer this question specifically, let us turn to chapter three and consider how these percept-stages fit together.

Chapter 3
Time and Causes

> How rational is it to suppose that God, however he has left meaner goods and lower gifts to second causes, and in some sort in their power, yet should reserve this most excellent, divine, and important of all divine communications, in his own hands, to be bestowed immediately by himself, as a thing too great for second causes to be concerned in?
>
> — Jonathan Edwards[1]

Introduction

According to Edwards, '[God] causes all changes to arise *as if* all these things had actually existed in such a series in some created mind, and *as if* created minds had comprehended all things perfectly'.[2] Having already established that when Edwards talks about ideas in a series, he is rightly understood as endorsing a stage-theoretic account of persistence and that these stages are in fact divine-percepts

---

[1] "A Divine and Supernatural light", *WJE* 17:421–22 (emphasis added).

[2] "The Mind", *WJE* 6:354.

that are shared with created minds, we now come the question(s) about 'stage-intervals' and how Edwards thinks God puts together and organizes this series of stages and their content.

Now, when we talk about 'stage-intervals' we are talking about both the temporal duration or length of a given temporal stage or what is often called a 'temporal index', and what we might think of as instants between instants of time or the moment-to-moment temporal space between, as it were, temporal stages, if there even is such a thing. Technically speaking, the discussion about what I am calling stage-intervals has to do with the difference between *dense* and *discrete* accounts of time on the one hand, about which Edwards says little that is definitive, and divine and secondary causality on the other, about which Edwards says comparatively more. For this reason, following a brief word about dense and discrete time, we will spend the remainder of our exploration of Edwards' doctrine of continuous creation in this third chapter by bringing some clarity to Edwards' doctrine of occasionalism, which is a key to our understanding of 'stage-intervals'.

Dense or Discrete Time?

We recall that one (admittedly small, though not insignificant) part of the objection to the coherence Edwards' doctrine of continuous creation has to do with how long a created mind exists—whether they exist long enough to perform a moral action. Part of this claim has to do with whether temporal stages have a dense or a discretely ordered duration. The majority report claims that Edwards looked at the nature of temporal stages along a dense view of time.[3] Dense accounts of time look at temporal stages as duration-less intervals;

---

[3] Crisp, "How 'Occasional' was Edwards's Occasionalism", in *JEPT*, p. 67–68.

near-indistinguishable instants of time, of which there is a potentially infinite number.[4] So, when looking at any given mundane object across a densely ordered account of time—something, again, like Edwards' chocolate cupcake, to return to our previous analogy—there are a potentially infinite number of chocolate cupcake-stages; each one, a temporal counterpart of a chocolate cupcake (that is a lot of cupcakes). Carving up time in this dense way becomes a problem for Edwards because, so it is argued, he supposedly thinks that human beings persist through time similar to any other mundane other object, and therefore exist for no more than a duration-less instant (i.e., a 'moment'), which is not long enough for any person, save only for a divine person, to make a moral choice. This problem is relatively straight forward.

Now, it must first be said that attempts to measure what Edwards thinks a stage's temporal duration might be from what little he says about the subject is not a little challenging. This is because Edwards offers only subtle hints about this technical aspect of his metaphysics of time. For this reason, it seems to me altogether possible that Edwards understood time in discete terms.[5] Discrete accounts of time look at

---

[4] Assuming that objects like banana's are composed of material substance, Hawley argues that the nature of change requires that stages be as 'fine-grained' as possible, at one point referring to them at one point as 'instantaneous stages'. It is not clear to me that immaterial realist metaphysical assumptions about such mundane created objects like bananas, being only perceptions, likewise require this. See: Hawley, *How Things Persist*, p. 52.

[5] Edwards gives us what is a subtle clue, for example, to his understanding of these so-called stage-intervals in *Original Sin*, when he argues that, 'In [a] point of time, what is past *entirely ceases*, when present existence begins; otherwise it would not be past', "Original Sin", *WJE* 3:400. About this statement, in particular, I have three observations. First, by 'points of time', I think Edwards means a distinguishable slice of tensed time. Just how long a 'point of time' is, is not altogether clear from this statement or the context, of course. What is clear, I think, is that Edwards seems to believe that the duration of a time interval is long enough to be distinguishable

temporal stages as having more than mere instantaneous duration, thereby reducing the number of candidate stages a thing might have.[6] If not instantaneous, the difficulty facing the discrete theorist is one of demarcating the boundaries of a given stage's duration, which is, of course, no easy business. How long does one stage last before it is replaced by another? A second? A minute? An hour? A day? Scouring Edwards' works to find a definitive answer to such questions is a fruitless exercise. The real question for us is: if an answer—whether dense of discrete—is indiscernible, how is this even material to the debate about Edwards' doctrine of continuous creation? On an immaterial realist reading of Edwards' metaphysics, I don't think it would be. This question and answer effectively reframes the debate. For,

from another, perhaps lending support to a discrete account of time. But how long? Long enough to perform a morally responsibly act? Possibly. Compare this previous statement with Edwards' discussion of duration and the succession of time in "The Mind": 'Number is a train of differences of ideas put together in the mind's consideration in orderly succession and considered with respect to their relations one to another, as in that orderly *mental succession*. This mental succession is the succession of time. One may make which they will the first, if it be but the first in consideration. The mind begins where it will and runs through them successively, one after another. It is a collection of differences; for it is its being another in some respect, that is the very thing that makes it capable of pertaining to multiplicity. They must not merely be put together in orderly succession, but it's only their being considered with reference to that relation they have one to another, as differences and in orderly mental succession, that denominates it number. To be of such a particular number, is for an idea to have such a particular relation, and [be] so considered by the mind, to other differences put together with it in orderly succession. So that there is nothing inexplicable in the nature of number but what identity and diversity is, and what succession, or duration, or priority and posteriority is', "The Mind", *WJE* 6:372.

[6] I imagine an unrolled strip of 35mm film and how the 'negatives' of each 'still' photograph are linked together by a sort of blackish, translucent material. On a discrete view of time, the shadowy-black negative 'space between' each photograph represents discernible breaks in perceptible stages. Whereas, on a dense view of time, these 'negative' spaces are actually stages themselves, giving the appearance of being stitched seamlessly together as one continuously uninterrupted photograph of still separate images, despite their all being 'stills' in and of themselves.

what possible explanatory value does a dense or discrete theorist reading of Edwards' stage theory have if stages are nothing but percepts? Comparatively little, I think. For, if we think that Edwards construes created minds as existing apart from their own perceptions—like the actor who is both in the film and yet able to watch himself at its public theater debut—and if he thinks time and space are populated only by perceptions and not with created minds themselves, it does not seem to make a difference whether temporal stages are carved up as instantaneous duration-less intervals or whether they unfold by increments of a second, a minute or an hour. In other words, because Edwards thinks that created minds are real—existing moment-to-moment *across* temporal stages—and are not, like percepts that God is re-creating at every moment, then the problem of whether a created mind can be morally responsible amounts to no real problem at all. Whether an agent (a created mind) has percepts that 'last' for this or that duration of time is no obstacle to the issue of moral responsibility.

On this way of thinking about Edwards' stage theory, it does not follow from the argument which says that Edwards ordered time densely that his account of continuous creation is incoherent. Thinking about stage theory in terms of Edwards' immaterial realism also reframes the debate about his commitment to occasionalism.

On Occasionalism

To this point in the literature, a nearly inseparable conceptual link has been forged in the minds of many of Edwards' contemporary interpreters between his doctrine of continuous creation and his supposed purchase upon the idea that God is the singular causal agent, with the combined result, again, that Edwards finds himself on the side of doctrinal incoherence.[7] In other words, for some interpreters, it's occasionalism for Edwards all the way down, so to speak. To this I have basically no material objection. That is, I don't think we have any good reason for denying that Edwards' is an occasionalist of some sort. I have, instead, a formal objection. That is, my objection is to how Edwards' occasionalism has hitherto been construed in the literature. The question for us then is not whether Edwards believed in some version of occasionalism.[8] He did. Neither is the question whether Edwards believed in mundane or secondary causes. He did; something for which there is a (often ignored) trove of primary source support.[9] The question for us is how to bring clarity to

---

[7] Crisp, "Jonathan Edwards' Ontology: A Critique of Sang Hyun Lee's Dispositional Account of Edwardsian Metaphysics", *Religious Studies* 46 (2010), p. 11; see also idem, *JEMS*, pp. 131–32. It is interesting that Crisp points out that the sources Lee uses to make the case against Edwards' occasionalism are often those also used to prop up Sang Lee's widely influential interpretation of Edwards' supposed development of a Dispositional Ontology. For a helpful treatment of the differences between Crisp and Lee on these matters, see: Stephen H. Daniel, 'Edwards' Occasionalism" in Donald Schweitzer, ed., *Jonathan Edwards as Contemporary: Essays in Honor of Sang Hyun Lee* (New York: Peter Lang, 2010), pp. 1–14. A more extensive and comprehensive comparison of Lee and Crisp's findings about divine action is something that demands more attention.

[8] There are a variety of species of occasional causation. For a helpful historical account of occasional causation in the early modern and modern periods, see: Nadler, *Occasionalism: Causation Among the Cartesians.* The debate about the species of occasionalism that Edwards supposedly developed is by not means an open-and-shut case. There is still a great deal of work that needs to be done to make clear Edwards' position, for example, a significant challenge to the metaphysical assumptions that Crisp lays out in his interpretation of Edwards has yet to appear.

[9] There is considerable (more than one hundred occurrences) textual support, both public and private, that Edwards made logical room for secondary—or what he sometime calls 'natural'—causes. See e.g.: *WJE* 1:156–57, 451; 2:208; 5:145; 6:49; 13:478; 14:33, 214, 220; 17:26, 97, 359, 365, 409, 422; 18:89, 157; 19: 77, 466; 20:327–28; 21:57, 304; 23:207, 242; 24:235; 25:64,90, 274, 288; 26:205, It is additionally noteworthy, that, there may in fact be—clear differences in their metaphysics notwithstanding, based

the fact that Edwards somehow managed to *square* secondary and occasional causes—occasional causes being those for which God is the sole agent, and secondary causes being those which are attributed by God to some other agent, moral or otherwise.[10] In other words, what I am concerned with is how we make sense of places where Edwards affirms, on the one hand, that it is 'certain with me that the world exists anew every moment, that the existence of things every moment ceases and every moment is renewed', and then go on to affirm that 'God's constitution that some of our ideas shall be connected with

on a comparison of argumentative development and language—much more to the relationship that Edwards had with Ames on this very issue. Ames says, for example, that, 'All secondary causes are predetermined to some extent by the force of this [common] government. First, they are stirred to work by an influence or previous motion. Some such process is necessary to put into action that which was before only potentially in the creature (before the communication and maintenances of powers). Second, the causes are applied to the object towards which they work, Ezekiel 21:21, 22; 2 Samuel 16:10. Third, by force of the same government they are given order, i.e., limits and bounds are set to their action, Job 1:12; 2:6; 38:10. Some good results from their actions, Genesis 50:20', *Marrow* 1.9.25, p. 110. Such distinctions sound quite a lot like those which Edwards employs in various places when he talks about the distinctions between God's moral government.

[10] It is noteworthy that, according to Anderson, Edwards considered ten additional refinements (c. 1724–25) to the standard Aristotelian notion of an efficient cause (i.e. agent change); offering a clue into what we might call a 'thicker' account of Edwards' notion of mundane causation. Edwards says, 'What a cause, how we get a notion of it. In most natural things partial causes. 'Tis the proper effect of rain to be advantageous, the hurt by wetting accidental to it. 'Tis the proper effect of virtue to get a good name, accidental that it gets a bad one. Proper effect of God's Word to make a man better, an accidental to make him worse. 'Tis the proper Effect of God's Word to make a man better, an accidental that it softens. Of water to cool, accidental that it heats. The rays of the sun the next cause of corn's growing; the remote, the plowing the ground. The string is the next cause of the flying of the arrow, the powder of the bullet; remote, man's hand.... Light in the sun is the universal cause of light in the looking glass. Knowledge in the teacher is the universal cause of knowledge in the scholar. Holiness in God of holiness in man. The heat of the sun is the universal cause of plants' growing' (*WJE* 6:350, no. 6). There is yet a great deal more technical work to be done on Edwards' model of divine action.

others according to such a settled law and order, so that some ideas shall follow from others as their cause'.[11] The answer to this question is bound up with Edwards' immaterial realism as well as several subtle and interrelated distinctions about divine causation.

The first distinction, from which it seems like the other, more subtle ones follow, turns on Edwards' account of God's communication of himself to created minds. Edwards carefully explains that in the case of God's communicating divine knowledge to persons (minds), that it is paramount in the mind of God to act upon 'intelligent creatures' immediately (occasionally), rather than mediately (through some secondary causes). The next distinction Edwards makes is also quite clear, namely that God's intimate conservation of his creation is certainly not at odds with secondary causes. In that now famous sermon, *A Divine and Supernatural Light*, he says that

> 'Tis strange that men should make any matter of difficulty of it. Why should not he that made all things, still have something immediately to do with the things that he has made? Where lies the great difficulty, if we own the being of a God, and that he *created all things out of nothing*, of allowing *some immediate influence of God on the creation still*? And if it be reasonable to suppose it with respect to any part of the creation, 'tis especially so with respect to reasonable intelligent creatures; who are next to God in the gradation of the different orders of beings, and whose business is most immediately with God; who were made on purpose for those exercises that do respect God, and wherein they have nextly to do with God: for reason teaches that man was made to serve and glorify

---

[11] "The Mind", *WJE* 6:359; Compare with: "Miscellany" n. 125a, *WJE* 13:288.

his Creator. And if it be rational to suppose that God immediately communicates himself to man in any affair, it is in this. 'Tis rational to suppose that God would reserve that knowledge and wisdom, that is of such a divine and excellent nature, to be bestowed immediately by himself, and that it should not be left in the power of *second causes*. Spiritual wisdom and grace is the highest and most excellent gift that ever God bestows on any creature: in this the highest excellency and perfection of a rational creature consists. 'Tis also immensely the most important of all divine gifts: 'tis that wherein man's happiness consists, and on which his everlasting welfare depends. How rational is it to suppose that God, however *he has left meaner goods and lower gifts to second causes*, and *in some sort in their power*, yet should reserve this most excellent, divine, and important of all divine communications, in his own hands, to be bestowed immediately by himself, as a thing too great for *second causes* to be concerned in? 'Tis rational to suppose that this blessing should be immediately from God; for there is no gift or benefit that is in itself so nearly related to the divine nature, there is nothing the creature receives that is so much of God, of his nature, so much a participation of the Deity: 'tis a kind of emanation of God's beauty, and is related to God as the light is to the sun. 'Tis therefore congruous and fit, that when it is given of God, it should be nextly from himself, and by himself, according to his own sovereign will.[12]

This passage also confirms that Edwards thinks God's continuous creation of things describes his post-creation (i.e., conserving)

---

[12] "A Divine and Supernatural light", *WJE* 17:421–22.

activity, upon which he then introduces a division of two sorts of continuously creative acts. Let us call them *direct* and *indirect* acts.[13] Direct continuously creative acts appear to be those that Edwards thinks correspond to God's 'emanating' communications of himself to 'intelligent creatures' (i.e., created minds), whereas indirect continuously creative acts are those that Edwards thinks correspond to those causes (i.e., laws) that are designed by God to occur naturally to perceiving minds. I say 'continuously creative acts' because I think that the context of these previous statement warrants as much. What constitutes God acting directly is, as Edwards says, the communication of 'knowledge and wisdom, that is of such a divine and excellent nature' and 'a participation of the Deity' that results in the creatures glorification of God. What constitutes God acting indirectly through natural causes amounts to what Edwards calls 'meaner goods and lower gifts', about which he says nothing further in any great detail.[14]

---

[13] Edwards elsewhere describes what I am calling direct and indirect activity as God's 'arbitrary' and 'natural operations', about which, much has been made in the literature (See e.g.: Crisp, 'How "Occasional" is Edwards's Occasionalism?' p. 71ff). Accordingly, Edwards argues that, 'Of the two kinds of divine operation [arbitrary and natural], viz. that which is arbitrary and that which is limited by fixed laws, the former, viz. arbitrary, is the first and foundation of the other, and that which all divine operation must finally be resolved into, and which all events and divine effects whatsoever primarily depend upon. Even the fixing of the method and rules of the other kind of operation is an instance of arbitrary operation', "Miscellany", no. 1263, *WJE* 23:202. Wanting to avoid getting lost on the various protracted distinctions that Edwards then goes on to describe as part and parcel of these arbitrary and natural divine operations, I will continue with the direct-indirect distinction. For, it is not my intention to work out the intricacies of all that Edwards' thought about divine causation. Rather, it only my intent to point out and attempt to reconcile the fact that Edwards' occasionalism somehow made room for secondary causes, and what is more, to show, in light of Edwards' other metaphysical commitments that the combination of these notions was not a road-block, as it were, either to the coherence of Edwards' doctrine of continuous creation or his continuous Christology.

[14] This is not the only place Edwards makes this distinction. Compare with "Miscellany", no. 1263, *WJE* 23:201–12. There may also be something to this distinction

From what we have seen of Edwards' commitment to immaterial realism, two things occur to me. First, on Edwards' way of thinking, direct (occasional) divine activity is restricted to the creation and re-creation of the *perceptible* world, not to created minds.[15] This is what Edwards means when he says that '[God] causes all changes to arise *as if* all these things had actually existed in such a *series* in some created mind, and *as if* created minds had comprehended all things perfectly'.[16] Second, Edwards seems to think that secondary causes themselves follow laws that are programed, as it were, to perform this or that same sort of continuously creative action. Whether (for some reason) these secondary causes occur in concert with or altogether without God's immediate causal influence or activity is really beside the point. When God works in concert with those laws that he established, Edwards' calls them 'mixed operations', and when God acts in no way beyond the regular order of what Edwards sometimes calls the 'course of nature', causes follow from these established laws.[17] This is

---

as it pertains to Edwards' soteriology, particularly his account of regenerate and unregenerate knowledge. For more on this distinction see: Norman Fiering, *Jonathan Edwards's Moral Thought and It's British Context* (Chapel Hill, NC: University of North Carolina Press, 1981), ch. 2.

[15] In fact, this sounds quite similar to Berkeley, who argues, 'A proper active efficient cause I can conceive *none but Spirit*; not any action, strictly speaking, but where there is a Will. But this doth not hinder the allowing occasional causes (*which are in truth but signs*); and more is not requisite in the best physics, i.e. the mechanical philosophy. Neither doth it hinder the admitting other causes besides God; such as spirits of different orders, which may be termed active causes, as acting indeed, thought by limited and derivative powers. But for an unthinking agent, no point of physics is explained by it, nor is it conceivable', *Philosophical Correspondence with Johnson*, 'II. Berkeley to Johnson [November 25, 1729]', WGB 2:280-81 (emphasis added).

[16] "The Mind", WJE 6:354.

[17] "Miscellany", no. 1263, WJE 23:201–12. Edwards lists several, so-called, 'mixed operations', including among them, 'the laws of the operation of the minds of men' which seems to suggest that God and laws of nature ('at least, the laws of resistance and

why Edwards, on analogy, says, 'All dependent existence whatsoever is in a constant flux, ever passing and returning; renewed every moment, *as the colours of bodies are every moment renewed by the light that shines upon them*; and all is constantly proceeding from God, as light from the sun'.[18] It seems that Edwards thinks that these secondary causes—like gravity, for instance—have a mechanism that makes them function in a way that is God-like, in that they are re-creating the very percepts that they are tasked by God with performing.[19] In other words, what is

---

attraction or adhesion') are charged with the production or publication of (presumably continuously created) perceptible ideas (p. 205). He then goes on to classify 'two kinds of divine operation, viz. that which is arbitrary and that which is limited by fixed laws, the former, viz. arbitrary, is the first and foundation of the other, and that which all divine operation must finally be resolved into, and which all events and divine effects whatsoever primarily depend upon. Even the fixing of the method and rules of the other kind of operation is an instance of arbitrary operation. When I speak of arbitrary operation, I don't mean arbitrary in opposition to an operation directed by wisdom, but in opposition to an operation confined to and limited by those fixed establishments and laws commonly called the laws of nature. The one of these I shall therefore, for want of better phrases, call a natural operation; the other, an arbitrary operation', Ibid., 202.

[18] *WJE* 3:404 (emphasis added).

[19] See e.g.: Crisp argues that for Edwards, 'God creates "arbitrarily" [that is, according to his will], and conservation is an illusion: God recreates all things ex nihilo each moment, including the "laws" themselves, which appear to be physical constants at each index merely because God "arbitrarily" designs that they operate in such a fashion', "How "Occasional" is Edwards's Occasionalism?", p. 73. According to Edwards, 'the operation by which these things was done was not so absolutely, purely and unmixedly arbitrary as the first creation out of nothing. For *in these secondary operations*, or the works of what may be called a secondary, some use was made of laws of nature before established; such, at least, as the laws of resistance and attraction, or adhesion and vis inertiæ, that are essential the very being of matter, for the very solidity of the particles of matter itself consists in them. But the putting these particles into motion supposes 'em to exist. In the moving inert, resisting and adhering matter, there is use made of the laws of resistance and adhesion. They are presupposed as the basis of this secondary operation of God in causing this resistance, vis inertiæ, and adhesion to change place, and in causing the consequent impulses

continuously created is that which is strictly phenomenal; nothing but a sea of percepts, as it were.[20] There are, of course, a host of questions that follow from this sort of distinction, one of which is of primary interest to the debate about Edwards' account of occasionalism and the coherence of his doctrine of continuous creation.

Part of what characterizes the supposed incoherence of Edwards' doctrine is the idea that Edwards thought temporal stages, upon being re-created, were destroyed. For, Edwards says, "Tis certain with me that the world exists anew every moment, that the existence of things every moment *ceases* and every moment is renewed'.[21] Some have taken this to mean that 'past' temporal stages (or temporal parts, depending on the model of four-dimensionalism used to explain Edwards account of persistence), fall out of existence.[22] The implication here, were Edwards an anti-realist and were God re-creating minds every moment, is that minds are destroyed every moment. Were this the case it would be not an inconsiderable problem for Edwards, and sheds some light of the issues related to moral responsibility that have populated the literature related to this subject to this point.

This is to say nothing of the Christological problem. For it follows on this way of thinking, that the created mind of Jesus is destroyed every moment, re-created every moment, and hypostatically re-united

---

and mutual influences which is the end of those motions and dispositions of the situation of particles. So that *the creation of particular natural bodies*, as the creation of light, the creation of the sun, moon and stars, of earth, air and seas, stones, rocks and minerals, the bodies of plants and animals, *was by a mixed operation, partly arbitrary and partly by stated laws*', "Miscellany", no. 1263, WJE 23:204–5.

[20] It would certainly be an interesting project to square Edwards' doctrine of continuous creation—and all that he says about occasional and secondary causes—with his discussion of the so-called 'Images of divine things'.

[21] "Miscellany", no. 125a, WJE 13:288.

[22] Crisp, *Revisiting Christology*, p. 56.

to the Son every moment. And it is for these reasons and their apparently insuperable consequences that I think we ought to take issue with this reading of Edwards.

I think that by 'ceases', Edwards does not mean that past stages are destroyed or eliminated. This would undermine what I take to be Edwards' commitment to *eternalism*, which again is the idea that all stages or 'points of time'—past or future—are equally *real*, though not necessarily present.[23] Given what we have now seen about the function of Edwards' immaterialism and occasionalism, I think what he means when the past 'entirely ceases' is not something referring to minds. Certainly minds don't cease to exist. Neither, strictly speaking, do their ideas. 'Entirely ceases' might more helpfully be referred to 'archived'. That is, these stages are re-indexed as an event upon which God alone has comprehensive access—his seeing all from eternity—and which he gives created minds access to by the service of their memory.

To tweak our actor-film analogy slightly, think of those now largely-obsolete 35mm film carousel-projectors that hold 'slides' of individuated negative photographs. When the carousel-projector operator pushes a remote button, an individual slide is moved into a position in front of the light, displaying the image for all to see.[24] When the operator activates the carousel-projector to change to the next slide, the

---

[23] Copan and Craig seem to think that if the doctrine of divine conservation (i.e., Providence) is construed as continuous creation, the idea of original creation (i.e., Temporal beginning) is undermined, if not, made altogether irrelevant; see: Paul Copan and William Lane Craig, *Creation out of Nothing: A Biblical, Philosophical and Scientific Exploration* (Grand Rapids: Baker Academic, 2004), pp. 13, 148–50. One 'condition' it seems is the 'published' (to borrow a term from Bishop Berkeley) existence of created minds as so-called 'notions'. Prior to created minds being notions on Berkeley's view, such minds are merely ideas in the divine mind.

[24] This analogy sounds very much like a 'moving-spotlight' account of temporal persistence, a recent and novel defense of which stage theory is a possible explanation is

former slide moves into a imperceptible (though still extant) position. The slide remains. It simply is no longer in our view. This is what I mean by 'archived'. Edwards elsewhere explains something like what I have described here, saying,

> '"Pastness," if I may make such a word, is nothing but a *mode of ideas.* This mode perhaps is nothing else but a certain veterascence attending ideas. The mind judges [pastness] by nothing but the difference it observes in the idea itself, which alone the mind has any notice of. But it judges distance by a particular mode of indintinctness, *as has been said before.* So it is which respect to distance, by a certain peculiar inexpressible mode of facing and indistinctness which I call veterascence'.[25]

Archiving is what I take as the 'mode of ideas' to which Edwards refers. These are simply ideas that have a status of non-present perceptions. Of course, these perceptions are present to the mind of God, who as Edwards says, 'sees all from eternity', but are no longer 'present' us. These temporal stages still exist. That is, these perceptions exist as stages where the perceptions are instantiated exist. But they exist only by one's recollected memory of them, whereas for God, they are in full divine view.

Now, to this point, in these first three chapters, it has been my aim to offer up an alternative reading of Edwards immaterialism, stage theory, and occasionalism, all in service of clarifying what Edwards

---

given in Ross P. Cameron, *The Moving Spotlight: An Essay on Time and Ontology* (Oxford: Oxford University Press, 2015), pp. 152–54.

[25]"The Mind", *WJE* 6:372. It is not an insignificant clue that, according to Anderson, Edwards' reference to 'as been said before' is a reference to Berkeley's *New Theory of Vision*, (*WJE* 6:372, n. 1).

says about continuous creation and all this, as it relates to Edwards' theological anthropology of created minds. Having now arrived at the understanding that the metaphysics underpinning Edwards' doctrine of continuous creation is in fact coherent, we have now reached the point at which we can look with greater precision, clarity and accuracy into Edwards' so-called continuous Christology.

Chapter 4
Thirty Years a Man

Such was the love of the Son of God to the human nature, that he desired a most near and close union with it, something like the union in the persons of the Trinity, nearer than there can be between any two distinct [beings]. This moved him to make the human become one with him, and himself to be one of mankind that should represent all the rest, for Christ calls us brethren and is one of us. How should [we] be encouraged, when we have such a Mediator!

— Jonathan Edwards[1]

Introduction

UPON THE BROADER metaphysical foundation just laid let us now consider three corresponding points of interest to Edwards' continuous Christology, beginning with the created mind of Jesus of Nazareth as a real substance and its relation to other created minds and to the Son. After this we will consider the impact of stage theory on

---

[1] "Miscellany" no. 183, *WJE* 13:529–30.

the mind and body of the God-man. Third and finally we will look at the causal structure that is at play for the God-man and, more specifically, the necessity of his being a morally responsible representative for humanity.

Christological Anthropology

Of the various models of the hypostatic union on offer in contemporary philosophical theology, Edwards' thinking falls most naturally into a category that is sometimes called an 'abstract-nature' Christology.[2] On the abstract-nature view of hypostasis, the Son assumes a set of properties— better still, ideas, in view of Edwards' immaterial realism—that together compose a human nature.[3] Now, it must be

---

[2] For more on Edwards' doctrine of hypostasis and some of the finer points of his 'abstract nature Christology', see: Hamilton, "Jonathan Edwards, Hypostasis, Impeccability, and Immaterialism", *Neue Zeitschrift für Systematische Theologie und Religionsphilosophie* 58:2 (June 2016): 1–23

[3] For some recent and helpful discussion about abstract-nature Christology, see: Tim Pawl, *In Defense of Conciliar Christology: A Philosophical Essay* (Oxford: Oxford University Press, 2016), ch. 2. These properties would be (minimally) things like 'having a human soul (or mind)' and 'having a human body' (in other words, that which is necessary and sufficient conditions for being human). Whether Edwards thinks that such properties belong to a particular human nature that would have otherwise been born to Mary, had the Son not, by the Spirit, assumed them to himself—properties like 'being born in Bethlehem' or 'being the carpenter's son' or 'being of Nazareth'— is not something about which he makes a particular claim that I am aware of. This is in categorical contrast to what is often called the 'concrete-nature' account of hypostasis, which says that the Son assumes a concrete particular, in this case, a soul-body composite of some sort, which most say consists of an immaterial soul that is somehow united to a material body, both of which are distinct, property-bearing substances that the Son personalizes. It is worthy of noting that there is what appears to be at least some evidence that might possibly be marshaled to support a concrete-nature reading of Edwards' doctrine of Hypostasis. See e.g.: 'Miscellany n. 738', *WJE* 18:364. Compare with "Miscellany" n. 513, where Edwards argues, 'It seems to me reasonable to suppose, that that which the man Christ Jesus

said from the outset of the ensuing discussion that any attempt to cram Edwards' thinking about such things into these contemporary philosophical categories runs some pretty significant anachronistic risks.[4] That said, what we need to get greater clarity about concerning Edwards' continuous Christology is a working understanding of the anthropology that Edwards deploys in service of hypostasis. Thus, using the precision of contemporary Christological categories is a helpful move and borrowing from elements from arguments I have

had his divine knowledge by, that he had his union with the divine Logos by. For doubtless, this union was some union of the faculties of his soul; but Christ had his divine knowledge by the Holy Ghost. Acts 1:2, "After that he through the Holy Ghost had given commandments unto the apostles."' Edwards was in the habit of discussing both his theological and philosophical speculations in what called 'the old way', namely, the way that doesn't expressly take into account his idealism.

[4] Models of the hypostatic union of this sort are often referred to in the literature as 'parts Christologies,' of which there are two principal species: two-part and three-part Christologies. For some helpful and further detailed discussion of so-called 'parts Christologies', see: Richard Cross, "Parts and properties in Christology", in M.W.F. Stone (ed.), *Reason, Faith and History: Philosophical Essays for Paul Helm* (Aldershot: Ashgate, 2008), pp. 177–92. Now, the Son's assumption and union with a human nature, where the Son bears the properties of human nature is an example of what is some concrete-nature theorists call a 'two-part Christology'. This is because the abstract-nature view unfolds along as similar metaphysical storyline as the two-part concrete-nature account, the sole difference between it and the concrete-nature account being that rather than assuming a composite substance in the form of a human nature consisting of an immaterial soul and a material body, the Son assumes a particular set of properties that compose his individual and common—common to all humanity—human nature. Now, if we press in a little more we see that Edwards' version of abstract-nature hypostasis is I think, also a version of a two-part Christology, in that the Son himself is an immaterial 'substance' (what Edwards calls an 'uncreated mind') who assumes—takes ownership of—an immaterial soul or mind in the form of the man Jesus of Nazareth (whom Edwards would describe as a 'created mind'), whose body is also immaterial, that is, not composed of material substance. In effect, the human nature of Christ is a mind, provided the idea of Christ's body is a perception that this nature also has, which of course, it does.

made elsewhere, I take the following set of propositions as filling out some of the basics of Edwards' Christological anthropology:

1. A complete human nature consists of a created mind and body, rightly related.

2. Created human minds are immaterial substances.

3. Rightly related bodies to created minds are merely physical.

4. Physical bodies are complex percepts in the uncreated divine mind that are immediately moment-to-moment communicated to created minds.

5. A created mind's proper function in an immaterial world requires a physical body.

6. The human nature of Jesus of Nazareth is a created mind with a physical body.

7. The human nature of Jesus of Nazareth is united (by the Spirit) to the Son of God, who himself either is uncreated mind or is an uncreated mind or has an uncreated mind.

8. The union of the uncreated mind of the Son to the created mind of Jesus of Nazareth is ideal—though not by perception; the Son's ideas are productive and not mediated to him by any sense, like taste, touch, smell, et cetera, and this somehow includes the idea of the created mind of Jesus.[5]

---

[5] I am grateful for Jim Spiegel who pointed out to me the altogether curious fact that for all their efforts to defend a top-to-bottom immaterialism, Edwards and Bishop Berkeley both offer little to no explicit explanation of how an uncreated mind (the Son) can produce not only ideas, but other minds.

9. Bound up in the generation of the created mind of Jesus of Nazareth is the creation of all other created minds and their ideas, including those ideas presented to the mind of Jesus of Nazareth.[6]

With these theses now before us, let us consider the three aspects of Edwards' continuous Christology that are at issue and correspond to the preceding revision to Edwards' metaphysics. This will be in large part an explanation of propositions 8–9. Because the matter of created minds as substances is among the more controversial claims about Edwards' metaphysics, I will spend the bulk of what remains addressing that specifically, giving less space to those matters which I think are less contentious and require less explanation.

Substantializing Human Nature: 'A Fusion Model'

In chapter one, I hinted at the idea that created minds are substances of some sort and that they are somehow bound up in or 'substantialzed' by the created mind of Jesus of Nazareth, who is the pattern for all human nature.[7] The idea of substantializing human nature is

---

[6] The uncreated mind of the Son does not require sensory knowledge, according to Edwards, like a created mind does. There is nothing standing between, as it were, an idea in the divine mind and complete knowledge of that idea. Accordingly, Edwards argues that 'Seeing the perfect idea of a thing is to all intents and purposes the same as seeing the thing; it is not only equivalent to the seeing of it, but it is the seeing it: for there is no other seeing but having the idea', *WJE* 21:118a.

[7] A somewhat similar proposal, namely, that the hypostatic union extends (eschatologically) to those united to Christ, has been recently developed in part and along Thomistic lines, by Tom Flint in "Molinism and Incarnation", in Ken Perszyk, ed., *Molinism: The Contemporary Debate* (Oxford: Oxford University Press, 2011), pp. 493–545.

intimately tied up with Edwards' doctrine of union with Christ.[8] For this reason, I want to briefly take up our discussion from chapter one, fixing upon the relationship between what Edwards calls the 'relative union' and the 'union of hearts' and more specifically, focusing on what Edwards means that the elect are 'parts of Christ'.

According to Edwards' account of the relative union, '[B]y that act of taking the human nature upon himself, he sufficiently in the sight of God and in the sight of angels *assumed the elect part of mankind into an union with himself*'.[9] The relative union is something that Edwards describes as an effect of the incarnation. That the Son assumes a human nature in the incarnation, Edwards explains, is predicated on an act of divine love, when he says that 'Christ loves the elect with so a great and strong a love, they are so near to him, that God looks upon them as it were as *parts* of him'.[10] This is the 'union of hearts' (from eternity). Notice that Edwards makes Christ's love of the elect equivalent to their being made 'parts of him'. Now, the 'union of hearts', unlike the relative union, is atemporal or as he says, 'from eternity'—it occurs prior to the first creation. Describing the link between the two unions, in Miscellany 769, Edwards intimates that

---

[8] The germ of this idea, namely, that Edwards thought Christ substantializes human nature appears in Joshua R. Farris, "Edwardsian Idealism, *Imago Dei*, and Contemporary Theology", in Joshua R. Farris and S. Mark Hamilton, eds., *Idealism and Christian Theology: Idealism and Christianity*, Vol. 1 (New York: Bloomsbury Academic, 2015), pp. 83–106. A more recently developed iteration of this idea appeared in Farris' paper, "Capturing Edwards' Substance in his Christology Anthropology", presented at the national meeting of the *Evangelical Theological Society* (Fall, 2016).

[9] *WJE* 14:403 (emphasis added). For more on Edwards' discussion of the relative union, see: *WJE* 25:231; Sermon Series II, 1747, n. 879; 2 Cor 5:8, *WJEO* 65; Sermon Series II, 1749, n. 932; John 6:54, WJEO 67; Sermon Series II, 1750, n. 952; 1 Cor 10:17a, *WJEO* 68.

[10] *WJE* 14:404-5 (emphasis added).

we are elected in Christ, as we are elected in his election. For God having in foreknowledge given us to Christ, he thenceforward beheld us as members or *parts of him*; and so ordaining the head to glory, he therein ordained the members to glory. Or, in destining Christ to eternal life, *he destined all parts of Christ to it also*, so that we are appointed to eternal life in Christ, being in Christ his *members from eternity*.[11]

With this, we come up against three questions. First, how does Edwards see that the Son is united to the elect portion of humanity in the incarnation, that is, to elect human nature, *en masse*? Second, how does Edwards see that this union is established both from eternity and is yet somehow executed at a particular temporal stage in the life of the Christ (presumably at the incarnation)? Third, how does Edwards see that the love of the Son to his human nature (and all those elect bound up in it) or to human nature in general is equivalent to those human natures being 'parts' of him? What Edwards means by 'parts' is the key.

What Edwards means by 'parts of Christ' has, I think, to do with the relationship that the created mind of Jesus of Nazareth and all other elect created minds bear to temporal stages. Created minds, we have previously established, are on Edwards' way of thinking, substances in some attenuated or shadowy sense. This includes, of course, the created mind of the man, Jesus of Nazareth, who exists as an idea of the Son from eternity, and who nevertheless appears, as the Apostle says, 'at the fulness of time' (Galatians 4.4). What I think Edwards assumes is that these diminished substances (i.e., created minds) somehow (perhaps as ideas in the divine mind) exist a-temporally

---

[11] "Miscellany" no. 769, *WJE* 13:418 (emphasis added).

with the Son who as we have just seen, substantializes them by virtue of their particular relationship or union with him and his union with the created mind of Jesus. In this way, the elect portion of created minds can exist 'from eternity', namely, by being an idea of human nature, along with the man, Jesus, in the uncreated mind of the Son, all of whom appear at some point or temporal stages. In a way similar to Berkeley, Edwards seems to think these ideas in the mind of God are eventually, as Berkeley says, 'published'. Let us call this relationship 'collective-*nature-perichoresis*' or the interpenetration of Christ's human nature *en masse* with those to whom he is a-temporally united.[12]

Nature-perichoresis (in contrast to the so-called person-perichoresis of Trinitarian relations) is the doctrine that has historically attempted to describe the relationship of the divine and human natures of the God-man.[13] Nature-perichoresis has to do with how one nature that is divine is united with another nature that is human, (not so much with how contradictory properties might be attributed to one or the other nature).[14] We need not get bogged-down with trying to develop a full-orbed discussion of nature-perichoresis here. What we need is a rough and ready idea of how something like collective-

---

[12] Helm calls this 'linear *collective* responsibility', based on what philosophers call a temporal parts reading of Edwards' four-dimensionalism; see: Paul Helm, "Locke and Edwards on Personal Identity", in Paul Helm and Oliver D. Crisp, eds. *Jonathan Edwards: Philosophical Theologian* (Aldershot: Ashgate, 2004), p. 56–57.

[13] For some additionally helpful discussion of both nature-perichoresis and person-perichoresis, see: Charles C. Twombly, *Perichoresis and Personhood: God, Christ, and Salvation in John of Damascus* (Eugene, OR: Pickwick Publications, 2015); Randall Otto, "The Use and Abuse of Perichoresis in Recent Theology" in *Scottish Journal of Theology* 54 (2001): 366–84; Richard Cross, "Christological Predication in John of Damascus" in *Medieval Studies* 62 (2000): 69–124.

[14] For some helpful discussion of the differences associated with the doctrine of perichoresis and doctrine of the communication of attributes, see: Crisp, "Problems with Perichoresis", *Tyndale Bulletin* 56.1 (2005): 119–40.

nature-perichoresis helps explain the relationship of the 'parts' of Christ and what this has to do with at the intersection of Edwards' notion of relative union and the union of hearts.[15]

Perhaps the best way to explain what I mean by collective-nature-peri-choresis is in terms of what I will more accurately refer to as *Fusion theory*. What I am calling Fusion theory is playing off of Michael Rea's suggestion that Edwards' hamartiology (and the transmission of sin in particular) is explained best by what he calls the *Fission theory*, according to which, at the moment of Adam's primal sin, Adam 'underwent fission, splitting into billions of people'.[16] For, as Edwards explains,

> My meaning, in the whole of what has been here said, may be illustrated thus: let us suppose, that Adam and all his posterity had coexisted, and that his posterity had been, through a law of nature established by the Creator, united to him, something as the branches of a tree are united to the root, or the members of the body to the head; so as to constitute as it were one complex person, or one moral whole: so that by the law of union there should have been a communion and coexistence in acts and affections; all jointly participating, and all concurring, as one whole, in the disposition and action of the head: as we see in the body natural, the whole body is affected as the head is affected; and the whole body concurs when the

---

[15] It is certainly worth noting that in chapters 31–43 of *Monologion*, Anselm hints at something close to what I am trying to develop here with collective-nature-perichoresis (see: Anselm of Canterbury, *The Major Works* (Oxford: Oxford University Press, 1998), pp. 46–51).

[16] Rea, "The Metaphysics of Original Sin", *Persons: Human and Divine*, p. 343–45; See also: Crisp, *JEMS*, chs. 4 and 5.

head acts. Now, in this case, the hearts of all the branches of mankind, by the constitution of nature and the law of union, would have been affected just as the heart of Adam, their common root was affected. When the heart of the root, by a full disposition committed the first sin, the hearts of all the branches would have concurred; and when the root, in consequence of this, became guilty, so would all the branches; and when the heart of the root, as a punishment of the sin committed, was forsaken of God, in like manner would it have fared with all the branches; and when the heart of the root, in consequence of this, was confirmed in permanent depravity, the case would have been the same with all the branches; and as new guilt on the soul of Adam would have been consequent on this, so also would it have been with his moral branches. And thus all things, with relation to evil disposition, guilt, pollution and depravity, would exist, in the same order and dependence, in each branch, as in the root. Now, difference of the time of existence don't at all hinder things succeeding in the same order, any more than difference of place in a coexistence of time.[17]

On the Fusion theory, the human nature of Jesus, presumably for Edwards at the moment of the incarnation, absorbs or reconstitutes the human nature of those whom he elects into himself (across all temporal stages), such that there is a property of Christ's human nature shared by all elect human nature. So, where in a way similar to the fracturing of humanity into Rae's 'billions of persons' that occurs across space-time at the temporal stage of the Fall, we might

[17] WJE 3:391, n.1.

say that there is a sort of reconstituting effect upon elect humanity (what Edwards goes on to describe in *Original Sin* as a 'moral whole' of humanity) such that elect persons (created minds) 'from eternity' who exist across different stages of space and time are brought into a collective-perichoretic-union with the human nature of the God-man; the incarnation being the trigger, as it were. This leaves open to question the relation that non-elect created minds bear to the human nature of Jesus. It may be that the perichoretic-union envisioned here has two stages, one that obtains at the incarnation and is effective for all humanity (including non-elect human minds) and another that obtains exclusively and soteriologically for elect human minds at the atonement where Edwards' 'legal union' is effective. While there may be some precedent for this based on our reasoning in chapter one, it is not entirely clear to me how Edwards made sense of the status of those human natures of non-elect minds. With this tension in mind, consider the following few observations.[18]

First, I do not think that Edwards thought that the uncreated mind of the Son and the created mind of Jesus of Nazareth, perichroetically-united together, formed another substance. The Son bears the human nature of Jesus as a property that is also, somehow a substance itself. Perhaps we might think of this relation as similar to the one that is shared by a *substance* and *substantive* dualist. Substance dualism, broadly speaking, is the idea that immaterial mind or souls and material bodies, both of which are distinct, property-bearing substances are also somehow able to communicate properties one to another.

---

[18] I am conscious of the fact that talk of indwelling and immaterialism together poses a problem because immaterial things have no extension; by definition they are no where. This is problematic from both the human and divine side of Edwards' Christological equation by virtue of the fact that both the uncreated mind of the Son and the created mind of Jesus are both immaterial substances. It is not clear to me at this point that Edwards was conscious of this problem.

Substantive dualism, on the other hand, is roughly, the idea that substances can consist of (at least) two distinguishable parts of a single concrete thing, one of which might be called a 'weaker substances', together which can also compose one thing.[19] However, to say that the created mind of Jesus of Nazareth to whom the Son is hypostatically united, exists in the divine mind as idea means that one sort of property-bearer (a created mind—Jesus) is also a property (of an uncreated mind—the Son). This is clearly a category confusion of two sorts of things: properties and property-bearers. Nevertheless, strangely, Edwards thinks that created minds somehow exist "within" and are "communications" of the divine mind, almost as if such minds are not simply property-bearers of those ideas that are communicated to them by God, but that they themselves are properties of the divine mind—ideas that God somehow has of himself. This is ironically in keeping with what we have seen thus far regarding Edwards' doctrine of union with Christ and human nature. This is nothing short of bizarre. It is not entirely clear what Edwards means by this.

Perhaps it might simply be best to say that Edwards conceived of created minds as existing in a sort of shadowy sense as the mental projections of the divine mind. He says as much in several places that 'all being is, in strictness only a *shadow* of [God's]'.[20] It may well be that this is what Edwards means when he describes the idea of 'self-union', which he says is something that occurs 'in pure love to others (i.e., Love not arising from self-love) [when] there's a *union of the heart* with

---

[19] For more on *substance* dualism, see e.g.: J.P. Moreland and Scott Rae, *Body & Soul: Human Nature & the Crisis in Ethics* (Downers Grove, IL: IVP Academic, 2000), ch. 2. For more on what I am calling *substantive* dualism, see e.g.: Eleanor Stump, *Aquinas* (New York: Routledge, 2003), ch.6 and Joshua R. Farris, *The Soul of Theological Anthropology: A Cartesian Exploration* (New York: Routledge, 2017), ch. 3.

[20] "The Mind", *WJE* 6:364 (emphasis added). See also: "Of Atoms", *WJE* 6:214 and "Miscellany" no. 108, *WJE* 13:279).

others; a kind of *enlargement of the mind,* whereby it so extends itself as to *take others into a mans self*.[21] Such statements, I think reinforce the idea that Edwards thought that the Son substantializes human nature; substances that are themselves (created) minds, existing independently of other minds, though notwithstanding their dependence on the divine mind.[22] Edwards' very explanation of the begottenness of the Son seems to include this sort of collective relation in human nature. Accordingly, he says, 'all God's ideas are only the one idea of himself, as has been shown, [then God's idea of himself] must be his essence itself. It must be a substantial idea, having all the perfections of the substance perfectly; so that by God's reflecting on himself the Deity is begotten, there is a *substantial image* of God begotten'.[23] In Miscellany 183, he offers a similar explanation, saying,

---

[21] *WJE* 8:589 (emphasis added). I am grateful to Kyle Strobel for pointing me to this reference.

[22] According to Edwards, 'Such was the love of the Son of God to the human nature, that he desired a most near and close union with it, something like the union in the persons of the Trinity, nearer than there can be between any two distinct [beings]. This moved him to make the human become one with him, and himself to be one of mankind that should represent all the rest, for Christ calls us brethren and is one of us. How should [we] be encouraged, when we have such a Mediator! 'Tis one of us that is to plead for us, one that God from love to us has received into his own person from among us. And 'tis so congruous that it should be so, and is also so agreeable to the Scripture, that it much confirms in me the truth of the Christian religion, "Miscellany" no. 183, *WJE* 13:329–30.

[23] "Miscellany" no. 94, *WJE* 13:257–58. Amazingly, Edwards later argues that, 'What insight I have of the nature of minds, I am convinced that there is no guessing what kind of union and mixtion, by consciousness or otherwise, there may be between them. So that all difficulty is removed in believing what the Scripture declares about spiritual unions—of the persons of the Trinity, of the two natures of Christ, of Christ and the minds of saints' ("Miscellany" no. 184, *WJE* 13:530). Edwards speaks as though there is some sort of equivalency in how we are to make sense of the nature of these various unions.

> Such was the love of the Son of God to the human nature, that he desired a most near and close union with it, something *like the union in the persons of the Trinity*, nearer than there can be between any two distinct [beings]. This moved him to make the human become one with him, and himself to be one of mankind that should represent all the rest, for Christ calls us brethren and is one of us. How should [we] be encouraged, when we have such a Mediator! 'Tis one of us that is to plead for us, one that God from love to us has received into his own person from among us.[24]

And again in *The Mind*, he writes,

> Seeing God has so plainly revealed himself to us, and other minds are made in his image, and are emanations from him, we may judge what is the excellence of other minds by what is his, which we shewn in love. His infinite beauty is his infinite mutual love of himself. Now God is the prime and original being, the first and the last, and the *pattern of all*, and has the sum of all perfection. We may therefore doubtless conclude that all that is the *perfection of spirits* may be resolved in that which is God's perfection, which is love.[25]

For Edwards, it seems then that he thinks that created minds are indeed substances by virtue of their relation to the human nature

---

[24] "Miscellany", no. 183, WJE 13:529–30.

[25] "The Mind", WJE 6:362–63. Compare with: 'Though the divine nature be vastly different from that of created spirits, *yet our souls are made in the image of God*: we have understanding and will, idea and love, as God hath, and *the difference is only in the perfection of degree and manner*', "Discourse on the Trinity", WJE 21:113.

assumed by the Son at the incarnation and for this reason, these created minds (including, of course, Jesus of Nazareth) are not re-created every moment as it has been elsewhere suggested. Jesus was not 'in constant flux'. His ideas, including those about himself, were. And this brings us around to the Christological impact of Edwards' stage theoretic account of persistence.

Chapter 5
Jesus, Time and Causes

When Christ appeared in the glory of his transfiguration to his disciples, with that outward glory, to their bodily eyes, which was a sweet and admirable symbol and semblance of his spiritual glory, together with his spiritual glory itself, manifested to their minds; the manifestation of glory was such, as did perfectly, and with good reason, assure them of his divinity.

— Jonathan Edwards[1]

Introduction

To this point I have argued, contrary to the majority report, that Edwards' stage theory proceeds on the immaterial realist assumption that created minds are substances and therefore 'constants', whereas ideas are merely percepts and are as Edwards says, 'in constant flux'. Minds, I argued, persist through (or across) time from moment-to-moment, whereas ideas do not. Ideas are simple and complex forms of perceptible objects that are created out of nothing every

---

[1] "Religious Affections", *WJE* 2:300.

moment by the divine mind in the form of (perhaps innumerable) perceptibly-indistinguishable temporal stages immediately presented to created minds by God. This, I argue, includes Edwards' thinking about the created mind of Jesus of Nazareth and all of his ideas, including those of himself.

Jesus Across Time

On Edwards' construal of hypostasis, the Son—the uncreated mind of God—assumes a created mind whose body is composed of percepts that are simply *made visible* or perceptible to other created minds, and that, by God's immediately presenting various simple and complex ideas of Jesus to those he encountered.[2] Speaking of the circumstances of the Son's visible appearance as the man Jesus of Nazareth, he says,

> The things that are here spoken of Christ are spoken of him as God-man, either so actually, or so by constitution or immutable undertaking and appointment. All things are from him as God-man, but he him[self] as God-man is from the Father. He is here spoken of as the image of the invisible God, i.e. the image of the Father. The Father is the author of his own image, as in Hebrews 1:3 he is called "the brightness or the shining forth of the Father's glory, and the express image of his person," which shows that *the glory of this image, as it exists in the view of the creature,*

---

[2] That Jesus of Nazareth 'makes visible' the Son of God is an idea is similarly developed by Bishop Berkeley and recently explained in Marc Hight and Joshua Bohannon, "The Son More Visible: Immaterialism and the Incarnation" in *Modern Theology* 26:1 (2010): pp. 120–48.

comes immediately from the Father, as light does from the sun, or as effulgence does from a luminary.[3]

So then, the strain felt by Mary at his birth; the disciples sight of his fearlessness before the demonic 'Legion'; the taste of his skin when Judas betrayed him with a kiss; the chilling sound of his dereliction; the smell of death at his tomb; for Edwards, all these were ideas of the God-man that (the Spirit of) the Son made perceptible to the minds of his parents, his disciples, his followers, even his executioners. The same is true and more interesting still for Jesus' perception of such things, that is, his self-perception. For, because the human nature of Jesus is for Edwards under the same metaphysical conditions as any other human nature, such things as the gritty-feel of the salt of the Dead Sea at his baptism; the pressure of John leaning on his bosom in the upper room; the scent of flowers in Gethsemane; the sting of the slap of the soldier's hands in the Praetorian; the taste of the gaul when put to his mouth as he hung on the cross—these were ideas that were presented to him by the (Spirit of) the Father, whereby he—by the Spirit of the Son, in his humanity—perceived the world.[4]

I do not think that what Edwards had in mind here is that at each of these moments (and perhaps at the infinite number of moments between each of them) that Jesus of Nazareth—both the mind and body—ceased to exist, only to be immediately re-created out of nothing at the next moment and instantaneously, hypostatically united

---

[3] "Miscellany", no. 958, *WJE* 18:238-9.

[4] In Miscellany 985, Edwards makes the following interesting distinction, 'All the works of God ad extra are wrought by Christ, excepting those that are immediately wrought *upon* or *about* Christ, or in which Christ himself is the effect or object, and *these are more immediately from God the Father*. All universally are by the Spirit, but the human nature of Christ and what belongs to it is by the Spirit as the Spirit of the Father; but all the rest are by the Spirit as the Spirit of the Son. The incarnation of Christ was the work of the Father', *WJE* 18:234 (emphasis added).

again to the Son. Rather, the Son assumes what the councils call a 'reasonable soul and body'—a human mind, whose body is but a collection of ideas in the mind (a claim which seems to still satisfy councilor conditions for orthodoxy)—and continuously maintains his hypostatic union with that human mind, despite the fact that the ideas that are presented to his various senses are ever-changing, perhaps including those of his sense of self.[5] For the sake of clarity, let us consider the sort of perceptible transaction that I envision is going on in Edwards' mind when he reads the narrative account of, say, Jesus' transfiguration.

A cursory look at his collected works shows that Edwards dedicates a relatively small amount of attention to the Transfiguration. The bulk of this attention is paid to Peter's account of the event (2 Peter 1:16–18) rather than any of the gospel narratives themselves, and is often and interestingly linked with his discussion of spiritual perception. For example, in Religious Affections, he writes,

> When Christ appeared in the glory of his transfiguration to his disciples, with that outward glory, *to their bodily eyes*, which was a sweet and admirable *symbol* and semblance of his spiritual glory, together with his spiritual glory itself, *manifested to their minds*; the manifestation of glory was such, as did perfectly, and with good reason, assure them of his divinity.[6]

Elsewhere Edwards offers the following explanatory refinement of the previous statement, saying,

---

[5] The Chalcedon Formula, *Documents of the Christian Church*, trans. Henry Betterson (Oxford: Oxford University Press, 1947), p. 73.

[6] "Religious Affections", *WJE* 2:300.

Spiritual light discovers the spiritual excellency and glory of God and Christ, and not merely an outward excellency. There is a great deal of difference between spiritual excellency and outward excellency. If we see or conceive of great beauty of the countenance, that is outward excellency. When we see the brightness and glory of the sun, that is an outward glory. So if we conceive of a being or countenance shining like the sun, why still it is but an outward glory. Spiritual excellency consists in the excellency of holiness, and truth, and justice, and grace, and such like. Therefore if a man seems to see God or Christ with great beauty of countenance and great outward glory, if that be all—if there be no sense [regenerate knowledge] of the spiritual excellency of God accompanying of it—that is nothing. If the body of man were never so beautiful, and shone brighter than the sun, that would be no spiritual excellency. When the disciples see Christ when he was transfigured, "and his face did shine as the sun, and his raiment was white as the light," that was not seeing the spiritual glory of Christ; though 'tis probably a great discovery of his spiritual glory [that] might accompany it.[7]

---

[7]"False and True Light", *WJE* 19:136. Previous to the comment, Edwards describes in some greater and illuminating detail the function of perception and the imagination, saying 'The imagination is the power of the mind whereby a man is capable of having the images or ideas of an outward thing in his mind. And when a person has some strong and lively idea or image of some outward thing impressed upon his mind, that is what is called an impression upon the imagination. Thus for instance, if a person has a lively impression of the countenance of his absent friend, that is an impression on his imagination; for the form of countenance is an outward [thing]. So if a person seems to have an impression or strong notion in his mind of a voice, or of some bright visible light, or of the pleasantness or nauseousness of the taste of anything, these things are impressions on the imagination; because all *these are all images of outward*

So, if this is what was seen by the disciples, *how* did they see it? The simple answer is as the statement above records, namely, that it was 'manifested to their minds'. The more complex answer is, as I already indicated, that 'The mere exertion of a new thought is a certain proof of God. For certainly there is something that immediately produces and upholds that thought; here is a new thing, and there is a necessity of a cause. It is not antecedent thoughts, for they are vanished and gone; they are past, and what is past is not'.[8] Recall that for Edwards, '[God] causes *all changes* to arise *as if* all these things had actually existed in such a series in some created mind, and as if created minds had comprehended all things perfectly. And although created minds do not, yet the divine mind doth, and *he orders all things according to his mind, and his ideas*'. Now, we certainly want to be careful not to inject Edwards' speculative metaphysics too deep into the vein of his exegetical labors (I say 'too deep' because, recalling Schweitzer's observation for previous chapters, Edwards did not insulate his exegetical inquiries from his metaphysical ones in several cases regarding continuous creation). So what was *manifested* to the disciple's minds? It was the moment-to-moment projection of ideas; divine ideas in fact, that is, ideas that God desired Peter, John, and James to know. These ideas not only established such empirical evidence for a truth claim, like, Jesus' garments are really white—what Edwards calls 'outward excellency'—they also further confirmed 'his divinity' to the disciples—knowledge that Edwards calls 'spiritual excellency'. In either case, the ideas 'manifested to their minds' in the event of Jesus' Transfiguration were, on Edwards' way of thinking, individual slices of time and space,

---

things that we perceive with our bodily senses. So any image or idea of any outward thing whatsoever, is an impression upon the imagination. But spiritual light don't consist in any impression upon the imagination, but is an exceeding different thing from it', p. 135.

[8] "Miscellany", no. 268, *WJE* 13:373.

each slice of which was uniquely created by God out of nothing—the grass beneath the disciples' feet, the light before their eyes, the fresh scent of the mountain air, the cool breeze, the stars in the sky, all the way down to the very vision of Jesus transfigured in light before them. So what this means then is that, in the 'moment' Jesus is praying, and 'his appearance was altered', God is not snuffing Jesus out of existence instantaneously and replacing him with another facsimile Jesus at the next moment. All that is 'changed' are the ideas presented to the disciples' minds. The same is true of the created mind of Jesus.

There appears to be no evidence to support the idea that Edwards distinguished, save for a matter of degree, between the way in which the created mind of Jesus operated in the created world from the operations of any other created mind. Jesus had ideas presented to him in the same way as any another created mind. To the contrary, comparing the human nature of the God-man with regenerate persons, Edwards clarifies, saying,

> The man Jesus becomes one person by a communion of knowledge and will; but *as in believers all divine knowledge is by the Spirit*—'tis by the Spirit that the knowledge of inspiration and prophecy is given, and 'tis by the Holy Ghost that the spiritual knowledge of all believers is given: "The Spirit searcheth all things, even the deep things of God" [1 Corinthians 2:10]—so, I suppose, *'tis by the Spirit that divine knowledge and consciousness is given to the man Jesus*. And so, as 'tis by the Spirit of God that a divine temper is given to men and angels, so I suppose 'tis by the Spirit of the Logos that the man Jesus hath the spirit and temper of the only begotten Son of God.[9]

[9] "Miscellany", no. 460, *WJE* 13:530.

If there is such an equivalence between the human nature of Jesus and any other human nature then it appears we have warrant for thinking that, as it pertains to our example of Transfiguration, Jesus himself under went changes to his body and in his mind similar to the manner of his disciples. The grass beneath the his feet, the light before his eyes, the fresh scent of the mountain air, the cool breeze, the stars in the sky, all the way down to the emissions of light coming off of his body and reflecting off the faces of his astonished followers, Jesus' experience of the world around him were composed of stages of simple and complex ideas brought immediately and repetitiously (i.e., continuously) before all his senses and all the while, his created mind remained in a constant state of perceptivity to observe and participate in them. The human mind of Jesus was not created and then recreated every moment. Every idea that came into his purview, however, was.

The next question, to which Edwards only hints at an answer, and to which we now turn, is whether the Son is the causal agent of the very percepts of his own human mind. The answer to this question orbits around Edwards' thinking about two things: occasional causation and Spirit Christology. Consider the following few observations.

Christ and Causes

Edwards' immaterial realism together with the augmented account of stage theory just laid out makes the robust occasionalism that Edwards is charged with adhering to, in my estimation, no problem at all. In fact, this sort of occasionalism follows from—and may well be entailed by—these other metaphysical commitments. God's being the sole cause of moment-to-moment continuously created *percepts* presents no obvious conceptual road blocks to the coherence of Edwards' doctrine of continuous creation. What then of Edwards' occasionalism and continuous Christology? If God is the sole cause of all percepts, does Edwards think that God is causing the percepts of the created mind that he assumed to himself in the incarnation? More to the point, is the Son continuously creating Jesus' ideas? Edwards does not answer this question directly. And yet, in Miscellany 1358, Edwards asserts that,

> 'Tis evident that the same WORD, the same Son of God, that made the world or gave it being, also UPHOLDS it in being and governs it. This is evident in part unto reason. For *upholding* the world in being and *creating* of it, are *not properly distinct works*. For 'tis manifest that upholding the world in being is the same with a *continued creation*, and consequently that creating of the world is but the beginning of upholding of it, if I may so say, the beginning to give the world a supported and dependent existence; and preservation is only continuing to give it such a supported existence.

Upon this Edwards goes on to consider the following interesting trinitarian implication, saying,

> But if these things are so, what shall we think of the upholding and government of the world while Christ was in his humbled state? [A]nd while an infant, when he had less knowledge than afterwards, when it is said that he increased in wisdom and stature, and [had] far less strength than he had afterwards? [W]hen we are told that he was wearied with his journey, wearied and his strength in a measure spent only with governing the motions of his own body? Who upheld and governed the world at that time? *Doubtless it will be said that God the Father took the world out of the hands of the Son for that time,* to

uphold and govern it, and *returned it into his hands again at his exaltation.* But is there any ground to suppose such a mighty change as this as to the Author of the universe, its having such different authors of its being and of all its properties, natural principles and motions and alterations and events, both in bodies and all created minds, for one, three, or four and thirty years, from what it had ever before or since? Have we any hint of such a thing? [O]r have we any revelation of anything analogous that ever has been? Has God ever taken the work of a creature out of its hand—that which is that creature's ordinary operation and care according to the ordinary course of things, out of that creature's hands—performing it precisely and exactly in the same manner that that creature did, as if the creature still went on in his own way, and then returned it into the hand of the creature again so that no interruption, not the least, should appear?[10]

In what remains of this lengthy entry, Edwards reasons that, in point of fact, the Son is in the end not divested of this sort of creative activity following the incarnation. He reasons that it is by the 'Spirit of the Son' that such activity occurs. This is Edwards' Spirit Christology. As this is something like opening pandora's box, in terms of the possible theological complexities, let us make only two observations here about the preceding statements.

That Edwards thinks a great deal about the Spirit's agency in the God-man, is evident from a variety of statements, like the following. Of the hypostatic union, Edwards writes,

---

[10] "Miscellany", no. 1358, *WJE* 23:608–9.

The bond of this union is the Holy Spirit. 'Tis manifest that the divine speeches that Christ uttered, and the divine works that Christ wrought, were by the Spirit of God. The divine words that he uttered, with which he taught the world divine things, and revealed God and the things of God to mankind, were by the Spirit of God. And the divine works that Christ wrought, wherein he manifested divine power, were by the Spirit of God. It will therefore follow that the union of Christ's human nature with the divine is by the Spirit of God. For those divine works that he wrought were his own works; they were not wrought by the Spirit, as the apostles and prophets wrought miracles by the power and in the name of another, but as wrought in his own name and by his own power. Though he was directed by the Spirit of God when and how to work those works, and was moved by the Spirit to work them, yet he wrought them as of his own wisdom and his own will. For those works of the divine power were his own no otherwise than as they were the works of the divine Logos, united to the human nature, or to the human understanding and will. But if that human understanding and will was directed and moved by the Holy Ghost, and yet it might be said to be done as of his own wisdom and will, *the Holy Ghost must in this act as a means of conveyance of the understanding and will of the divine Logos, to the understanding and will of the human nature, or of the union of these understandings and wills. And so, though it was of the motion of the Spirit of God, yet it was of himself, because these motions of the Spirit themselves were of himself, i.e. of his divine person, the person of the Logos, conveying and uniting the divine*

> *understanding and will, and so of the divine nature with the human.*[11]

Accordingly, Edwards seems to think that the Spirit is integral to the agency of the Son in the various internal and external activities of Jesus of Nazareth. The Son and Spirit both are actively at work; the Son is not simply a passive agent following his incarnation, as some might suppose. The Spirit's agency too, seems distinctly communicative. The Spirit (of the Son) prompts, motivates, discloses, and directs the Son's incarnate activity. This includes the provision of those perceptions that for the God-man are made sensible. But, if we compare this to Miscellany 709, where Edwards speaks more specifically about the activities of these two agents, and of particular interest to us, the Spirit's act of establishing the union of the Son to a human nature of Jesus 'out of nothing'. Edwards writes,

> It was necessary that the same person that acted as the principle or union between the manhood of Christ and the person of the Son, should make the manhood of Christ.

---

[11]"Miscellany", no. 766, WJE 18:412–13. Elsewhere, Edwards writes, 'The divine Logos is so united to the humanity of Christ that it spake and acted by it, and made use of it as its organ, as is evident by the history of Christ's life, and as it is evident he will do at the day of judgment. And this he does not occasionally once in a while, as he may in the prophets, but constantly, not by an occasional communication, but a constant and everlasting union. Now 'tis manifest that the Logos, in thus acting by the humanity of Christ, did not merely make use of his body as its organ, but his soul, not only the members of his body, but the faculties of his soul; which can be no otherwise than by such a communication with his understanding as we call identity of consciousness. If the divine Logos speaks in and by the man Christ Jesus, so that the man Christ Jesus in his speaking should say, I say thus or thus, and his human understanding is made use of by the Logos, and it be the speech of his human understanding, it must be by such a communication between the Logos and the human nature as to communicate consciousness', see: "Miscellany", no. 738, WJE 18:364.

For it must be by that person that acted as the principle of union that the human nature must be assumed, for assuming implies the uniting, and making is what belongs to assuming. This assuming may be considered as *one act, but having two effects*, viz. the being of the manhood, and his union with the person of the Son. Assuming is the making the human nature in the person of the Logos. It was the uniting something *out of nothing* (i.e. something as yet unmade) to him. Whatever Christ assumes into union to himself must be by that person that acts as the principle of union; and therefore, when something was to be *assumed out of nothing* into union to himself, the Logos or Word sent forth this constituent, or principle of assumption or unition, to assume it *out of nothing to himself.* But this implies making and uniting in one act, or making in union. If the making had been by one person and the unition by another, it must have been by two distinct acts because by two distinct agents; and the humanity would not, by him that made it, be *made out of nothing* into the Son, nor could the person that made it, be properly said to make the Word flesh.[12]

Are we to believe that Edwards thinks that the Spirit is making Jesus—his mind and body—out of nothing every moment, as in those places where he speaks of continuous creation? I don't think so. I think Edwards is here referring to the act of the person of the Spirit of God who established the union between the Son and man, Jesus Christ, which he then explains, consists of the formation or 'the making' of the human nature to whom the Son would then be united; also an

---

[12] "Miscellany", no. 709, *WJE* 18:333–35 (emphasis added).

act attributed to the Spirit. Interestingly, notice that Edwards calls this 'one act', referring to the person of Spirit as the singular actor. As he says, 'Assuming is the making the human nature in the person of the Logos', and that, 'out of nothing'. What this means then is that the Spirit is involved in the activity of creating the human nature of Jesus—what for Edwards is, as we have now clearly seen, a mind with what we might (for the sake of belaboring the effort to clarify what Edwards thinks) call a 'mental body', that is, a body conceived of ideas. This is why Edwards can speak of two creations, both of which are qualitatively different, the latter of which is continuous and restricted to perceptions.

Now, lest we think that Edwards contradicts himself, between this passage and the previous one, it appears that the 'one act' of the Spirit in assuming/making the human nature out of nothing is complimented by the Logos and his own 'principle or assumption'. In this way, the two passages—this one and the previous one—appear congruent in terms of how Edwards deploys the time-worn doctrinal principal of Trinitarian agency, namely, *opera trinitatis ad extra sunt indivisa* (the creative or external work of the persons of the Godhead are undivided). In a sense, the Son and the Father have an equal share, as it were, with the Spirit in the work of generating Jesus of Nazareth.[13] By assigning a concurrent action of the Son and the Spirit's work, Edwards cleverly (though perhaps not consciously) closes the door on the idea that the Son could have assumed something that was made by the Spirit (i.e., adoptionism). Notice, however, that Edwards does not reference the Father in this passage. Why? I think this is because Edwards thinks that this work of assumption is *peculiar* to the Spirit;

---

[13] I am grateful to Seng Kong Tan for pointing out to me the tension that remains in making sense of Edwards' commitment to the *opera trinitatis* principle and those places where Edwards claims that 'the incarnation was the work of the Father' ("Miscellany", no. 958, *WJE* 20:234–35).

peculiar in the sense that the Spirit is a sort of intermediary actor. This is why Edwards uses discriminating language like, 'Spirit of the Son' and 'Spirit of the Father'. And of course this is borne out by several examples in the previous passage.

Perhaps then the continuous creation of Jesus' ideas of himself terminate on the Spirit as the intermediary agent between the eternal Son and his assumed humanity. In the above passage, Edwards does intimate several times that he thinks that it is the Spirit who is the agent who 'assumes out of nothing'. Could it not also be the case that the Spirit performs this continuously creative work at every moment in the life of the God-man? In this sense, the assumption literally is what some theologians would describe as the sustaining of Christ's humanity by the Spirit (of the Son). Thus there would thereby be no qualitative difference in the Spirit's acting upon the man, Jesus, in the womb and his acting upon the man, Jesus, say, at the Transfiguration. The Spirit's activity would effectively swallow up the idea of the Spirit's continuously creative activity, because the self-consciousness of Jesus, to whom Edwards says the Spirit continually communicates, exists for no more than a moment before the Spirit is 'making' Jesus' reality anew at a subsequent moment. As Edwards sees it, the Spirit (of the Son) is the causal agent responsible for the systematic formation of numerically distinct, imperceptibly individualized temporal stages of Jesus' self-perception.

Conclusion

Truth, in the general, may be defined after the most strict and metaphysical manner: "the consistency and agreement of our ideas with the ideas of God."

— Jonathan Edwards[1]

WE HAVE COVERED a lot of ground, having at times come near the edge of the imponderable in our pursuit of greater philosophical and theological clarity about Edwards' doctrine of continuous creation and his continuous Christology. I argued that the metaphysical storyline on which Edwards' Christology unfolds—indeed, the metaphysical storyline itself—is quite different than what has appeared in the literature to this point. Specifically, in this treatise, I argued for an alternative reading of Edwards' account of substance(s), stage theory, and occasionalism, in order that I might show that Edwards' doctrine of continuous creation and his continuous Christology are, in fact, coherent. The combination of necessary revisions that I argued for include Edwards' commitment to:

   A– An immaterial realism, which means in this case (among several other things) that he thinks that all created human minds

[1] *WJE* 6:341–42.

are substances (of some sort), and that, by virtue of their being substantialized by their union with archetype of all human nature, namely, the human nature of Jesus of Nazareth.

B– A stage theoretic account of persistence, according to which stages are composed exclusively of ideas or perceptions with which created minds have only phenomenal interaction, whose duration is necessary and sufficient for the upholding of moral responsibility.

C– A species of occasional causation that is limited to God's causing perceptions rather than the intentions (i.e., the volition) of created minds.

Such revisions, as I have tried to show here, stem from a close reading of Edwards' philosophical speculations and what I think is the best explanation of the evidence derived from them, about which a great deal more could be said and certainly ought to be explored further. With these revisions in place, it seems that Edwards' doctrine of continuous creation is thus insulated from the charge of incoherence. By extension, Edwards' doctrine of continuous Christology receives some additional conceptual shoring. Summarily speaking, upon such broad metaphysical changes, Edwards continuous Christology amounts to his thinking that:

1– The humanity of Jesus is a real substance, composed of an immaterial mind and a body composed entirely of ideas presented to him by the Spirit.

2– The mind of Jesus persists through time by enduring moment-to-moment whereas the body of Jesus, like all other perceptible objects, is continuously created (by the Spirit) and re-presented *ex nihilo* to the mind of Jesus.

3– The Spirit (of the Son) is the principal actor and sole cause of this continuously creative activity, ever bringing the world into view for Jesus to perceive.

From all this, two things seem clear to me. First, I think we have a great deal more to learn about Edwards' Christology at large, much of which I think depends on the degree to which we can accurately understand his various metaphysical commitments. Second, I think that those discoveries about Edwards' doctrine of the person of Christ that have yet to be revealed will be made by digging much deeper, ironically, into his pneumatology; more specifically, his Spirit Christology.

Bibliography

Ames, William. *The Marrow of Theology*. Edited by John Dykstra Eisden. Grand Rapids: Baker, 1968.

Berkeley, George. *The Works of George Berkeley Bishop of Cloyne*, edited by A.A. Luce and T.E. Jessop, Vol 2. New York: Thomas Nelson and Sons, 1949.

Cameron, Ross P. *The Moving Spotlight: An Essay on Time and Ontology*. Oxford: Oxford University Press, 2015.

Copan, Paul and William Lane Craig. *Creation out of Nothing: A Biblical, Philosophical and Scientific Exploration*. Grand Rapids: Baker Academic, 2004.

Crisp, Oliver D. "On the Orthodoxy of Jonathan Edwards." *Scottish Journal of Theology* 67.3 (2014) 304–22.

———. "Problems with Perichoresis." *Tyndale Bulletin* 56.1 (2005) 119–40.

———. *Revisioning Christology: Theology in the Reformed Tradition*. Aldershot: Ashgate, 2011.

———. "Jonathan Edwards' Ontology: A Critique of Sang Hyun Lee's Dispositional Account of Edwardsian Metaphysics." *Religious Studies* 46 (2010) 1–20.

_____. "How Occasional was Jonathan Edwards' Occasionalism?" In *Jonathan Edwards: Philosophical Theologian*, edited by Paul Helm and Oliver D. Crisp, 61–76. Aldershot: Ashgate, 2003.

_____. *Jonathan Edwards and the Metaphysics of Sin*. Aldershort: Ashgate, 2003.

Cross, Richard. "Christological Predication in John of Damascus." *Medieval Studies* 62 (2000) 69–124.

_____. "Parts and properties in Christology." In *Reason, Faith and History: Philosophical Essays for Paul Helm*, edited by M.W.F. Stone, 177–92. Aldershot: Ashgate, 2008.

Daniel, Stephen H. "Edwards' Occasionalism." In *Jonathan Edwards as Contemporary: Essays in Honor of Sang Hyun Lee*, edited by Don Schweitzer, 1–14. New York, Peter Lang, 2010.

Descartes, Rene. "Third Meditation." In *Meditations on First Philosophy*, translated by Donald A. Cress. Indianapolis, IN: Hackett Publishing, 1993.

Edwards, Jonathan. *Freedom of The Will, The Works of Jonathan Edwards, Vol. 1*, edited by Paul Ramsey. New Haven: Yale University Press, 1957.

_____. *Religious Affections, The Works of Jonathan Edwards, Vol. 2*, edited by John E. Smith. New Haven: Yale University Press, 1959.

_____. *Original Sin, The Works of Jonathan Edwards, Vol. 3*, edited by Clyde A. Holbrook. New Haven: Yale University Press, 1970.

_____. *The Great Awakening, The Works of Jonathan Edwards, Vol. 4*, edited by C. C. Goen. New Haven: Yale University Press, 1972.

_____. *Apocalyptic Writings, The Works of Jonathan Edwards Vol. 5*, edited by Stephen J. Stein (New Haven: Yale University Press, 1977.

_____. *Scientific and Philosophical Writings, The Works of Jonathan Edwards Vol. 6*, edited by Wallace E. Anderson. New Haven: Yale University Press, 1980.

_____. *The Life of David Brainerd, The Works of Jonathan Edwards Vol. 7*, edited by Norman Pettit. New Haven: Yale University Press, 1984.

_____. *Ethical Writings, The Works of Jonathan Edwards Vol. 8*, edited by Paul Ramsey. New Haven: Yale University Press, 1989.

_____. *A History of the Work of Redemption, The Works of Jonathan Edwards Vol. 9*, edited by John F. Wilson. New Haven: Yale University Press, 1989.

_____. *Sermons and Discourses, 1720-1723, The Works of Jonathan Edwards Vol. 10*, edited Wilson H. Kimnach. New Haven: Yale University Press, 1992.

_____. *Typological Writings, The Works of Jonathan Edwards Vol. 11*, edited by Wallace E. Anderson and David Watters. New Haven: Yale University Press, 1993.

_____. *Ecclesiastical Writings, The Works of Jonathan Edwards Vol. 12*, edited by David D. Hall. New Haven: Yale University Press, 1994.

_____. *The "Miscellanies": Nos. a-z, aa-zz, 1-500, The Works of Jonathan Edwards Vol. 13*, edited by Thomas A. Schafer. New Haven: Yale University Press, 1994.

_____. *Sermons and Discourses, 1723-1729, The Works of Jonathan Edwards Vol. 14*, edited by Kenneth P. Minkema. New Haven: Yale University Press, 1997.

_____. *Notes on Scripture, The Works of Jonathan Edwards Vol. 15*, edited by Stephen J. Stein. New Haven: Yale University Press, 1998.

_____. *Letters and Personal Writings, The Works of Jonathan Edwards Vol. 16*, edited by George S. Claghorn. New Haven: Yale University Press, 1998.

_____. *Sermons and Discourses 1730-1733, The Works of Jonathan Edwards Vol. 17*, edited by Mark Valeri. New Haven: Yale University Press, 1999.

_____. *The "Miscellanies": Nos. 501-832, The Works of Jonathan Edwards Vol. 18*, edited by Ava Chamberlain. New Haven: Yale University Press, 2000.

_____. *Sermons and Discourses 1734-1738, The Works of Jonathan Edwards Vol. 19*, edited by M. X. Lesser. New Haven: Yale University Press, 2001.

_____. *The "Miscellanies": Nos. 833-1132, The Works of Jonathan Edwards Vol. 20*, edited by Amy Plantinga-Pauw (New Haven: Yale University Press, 2002.

_____. *Writings on the Trinity, Grace and Faith, The Works of Jonathan Edwards Vol. 21*, edited by Sang Hyun Lee. New Haven: Yale University Press, 2002.

_____. *Sermons and Discourses 1739-1742, The Works of Jonathan Edwards Vol. 22*, edited by Harry S. Stout and Nathan O. Hatch. New Haven: Yale University Press, 2003.

_____. *The "Miscellanies": Nos. 1153-1360, The Works of Jonathan Edwards Vol. 23*, edited by Douglas A. Sweeney. New Haven: Yale University Press, 2004.

_____. *The Blank Bible, The Works of Jonathan Edwards Vol. 24*, edited by Stephen J. Stein. New Haven: Yale University Press, 2006.

_____. *Sermons and Discourses, 174301758, The Works of Jonathan Edwards Vol. 25*, edited by Wilson H. Kimnach. New Haven: Yale University Press, 2006.

_____. *Catalogue of Books, The Works of Jonathan Edwards Vol. 26*, edited by Peter J. Theusen. New Haven: Yale University Press, 2008.

Farris, Joshua R. *The Soul of Theological Anthropology: A Cartesian Exploration*. New York: Routledge, 2017.

_____. "Edwardsian Idealism, Imago Dei, and Contemporary Theology." In *Idealism and Christian Theology: Idealism and Christianity*, Vol. 1, edited by Joshua R. Farris and S. Mark Hamilton, 83–106. New York: Bloomsbury Academic, 2015.

Fiering, Norman. *Jonathan Edwards's Moral Thought and It's British Context*. Chapel Hill, NC: University of North Carolina Press, 1981.

Flint, Thomas. "Molinism and Incarnation." In *Molinism: The Contemporary Debate*, edited by Ken Perszyk, 493–545. Oxford: Oxford University Press, 2011.

Freddoso, Alfred J. "God's General Concurrence with Secondary Causes: Why Conservation is Not Enough." *Philosophical Perspectives* 5 (1991) 553–58.

_____. "Medieval Aristoteleanism and the Case against Secondary Causation in Nature." In *Divine and Human Action: Essays in the Metaphysics of Theism*, edited Thomas V. Morris, 74–118. Ithaca: Cornell University Press, 1988.

Hamilton, S. Mark "Jonathan Edwards on the Election of Christ." *Neue Zeitschrift für Systematische Theologie und Religionsphilosophie* 58:6 (December 2016) 1–25.

_____. 'Jonathan Edwards, Hypostasis, Impeccability, and Immaterialism.' *Neue Zeitschrift für Systematische Theologie und Religionsphilosophie* 58:2 (June 2016) 1–23.

Hawley, Katherine. *How Things Persist*. Oxford: Oxford University, 2001.

Helm, Paul. "John Locke and Jonathan Edwards on Personal Identity." In *Jonathan Edwards: Philosophical Theologian*, edited by Paul Helm and Oliver D. Crisp, 45–60. Aldershot: Ashgate, 2004.

Hight, Marc and Joshua Bohannon. "The Son More Visible: Immaterialism and the Incarnation." *Modern Theology* 26:1 (2010) 120–48.

Hudson, Hud. *The Fall and Hypertime*. Oxford: Oxford University Press, 2014.

Kvanvig, Jonathan L. and Hugh J. McCann. "The Occasionalist Proselytizer: A Modified Catechism." *Philosophical Perspectives* 5 (1991) 587–615.

_____. "Divine Conservation and the Persistence of the World." In *Divine and Human Action: Essays in the Metaphysics of Theism*, edited Thomas V. Morris, 13–49. Ithaca: Cornell University Press, 1988.

Marsden, George. *Jonathan Edwards: A Life*. New Haven: Yale University Press, 2004.

McDonald, Scott. 'What is Philosophical Theology?' In *Arguing About Religion*, edited by Kevin Timpe, 17–29. New York & London: Taylor and Francis, 2009.

Muller, Richard A. *Post Reformation Reformed Dogmatics: The Rise and Development of Reformed Orthodoxy, ca. 1520 to ca. 1725, Vol. 3: The Divine Essence and Attributes*. Grand Rapids. MI: Baker, 2003.

Moreland, J.P. and Scott Rae. *Body & Soul: Human Nature & the Crisis in Ethics*. Downers Grove, IL: IVP Academic, 2000.

Nadler, Steven. *Occasionalism: Causation Among the Cartesians*. Oxford: Oxford University Press, 2011.

Otto, Randall. "The Use and Abuse of Perichoresis in Recent Theology." *Scottish Journal of Theology* 54 (2001) 366–84.

Pawl, Tim. *In Defense of Conciliar Christology: A Philosophical Essay*. Oxford: Oxford University Press, 2016.

Pessin, Andrew. "Does Continuous Creation Entail Occasionalism? Malebranche (and Descartes)." *Canadian Journal of Philosophy* 30 (2000) 413–40.

Quinn, Philip. "Divine Conservation, Secondary Causes, and Occasionalism." In *Divine and Human Action: Essays in the Metaphysics of Theism*, edited by Thomas V. Morris, 50–73. Ithaca: Cornell University Press, 1988.

Rea, Michael C. "The Metaphysics of Original Sin." In *Persons: Human and Divine*, edited by Peter van Inwagen and Dean Zimmerman, 314–56. Oxford: Oxford University Press, 2007.

———. "Four-Dimensionalism." In *The Oxford Handbook of Metaphysics*, edited by Michael J. Loux and Dean W. Zimmerman, 246–80. New York: Oxford University, 2003.

Rehman, Sebastian. "Towards a Solution to the 'Perennially Intriguing Problem' of the Sources of Jonathan Edwards' Idealism." *Jonathan Edwards Studies* 5:2 (2015) 138–55.

Roberts, John Russell. *Metaphysics for the Mob: The Philosophy of George Berkeley*. Oxford: Oxford University Press, 2007.

Schweitzer, William M. *God is a Communicative Being: Divine Communicativeness and Harmony in the Theology of Jonathan Edwards*. New York: T&T Clark, 2012.

Skow, Bradford. *Objective Becoming*. Oxford: Oxford University Press, 2015.

Stump, Eleanor. *Aquinas*. New York: Routledge, 2003.

Tan, Seng-Kong. *Fullness Received and Returned: Trinity and Participation in Jonathan Edwards* (Minneapolis, MN: Fortress Press, 2014).

———. "Trinitarian Action in the Incarnation." In *Jonathan Edwards as Contemporary: Essays in Honor of Sang Hyun Lee*, edited by Don Schweitzer, 127–50. New York, Peter Lang, 2010.

Trickett, Greg "Realist Conception of Truth." In *Idealism and Christianity, Vol. 2: Idealism and Christian Philosophy*, edited by James S. Spiegel and Steve Cowan, 29–50. New York: Bloomsbury Academic, 2016.

Turretin, Francis. *Institutes of Elenctic Theology*, edited by James Dennison Jnr., translated by George Musgrave Giger, Phillipsburg, NJ.: Presbyterian and Reformed, 1992–1997.

Twombly, Charles C. *Perichoresis and Personhood: God, Christ, and Salvation in John of Damascus*. Eugene, OR: Pickwick Publications, 2015.

www.ingramcontent.com/pod-product-compliance
Lightning Source LLC
Chambersburg PA
CBHW051946160426
43198CB00013B/2326